CW00505172

ANCIENT SCIENCE AND TECHNOLOGY FROM ETHIOPIA AND THE REST OF AFRICA

ANCIENT SCIENCE AND TECHNOLOGY FROM ETHIOPIA AND THE REST OF AFRICA

BY

Robin Walker

&

John Matthews

REKLAW EDUCATION LIMITED
London (U.K.)

First published in 2021 by Reklaw Education

Copyright © Reklaw Education 2012, 2016

All rights reserved. No part of this publication may be reproduced, stored in a retrieval system, or transmitted by any means, without the prior permission in writing from the publisher, nor be otherwise circulated in any form of binding or cover other than that in which it is published and with a similar condition including this condition being imposed on the subsequent purchaser.

CONTENTS

Figure 1. His Excellency, Mr Hailemariam Desalegn, former Prime Minister of Ethiopia.

PREFACE BY THE FORMER PRIME MINISTER OF ETHIOPIA, HIS EXCELLENCY, MR HAILEMARIAM DESALEGN

Mastery of the latest developments in science and technology are key to Ethiopia's continued progress as a complex nation. African American technology historian, Keith C. Holmes, lists some of the Ethiopian scientists and engineers who received patents for new technological developments. Engineer, Ayana Birru, received a patent from London, England, on 9 August 1932. He invented a typewriter adapted for use in Ethiopian languages. Tessema Dosho Shifferaw invented the billion-dollar generating "Bowflex" and "Selectech" exercise equipment trademarks. His company, Dosho, specialises in exercise equipment. He received patents from 1986 to 2016. Some of his patents are for geothermal energy generators. Dr Dagnachew Birru, an artificial intelligence pioneer, received 54 patents including a frequency-domain equalizer for terrestrial digital TV reception and ATSC digital television systems. Some of his patents were assigned to Koninklijke Philips Electronics, Netherlands, from 1999 to 2007. Among the others to distinguish themselves are the pathobiologist Professor Aklilu Lemma, computer scientist Professor Rediet Abebe, and the NASA space pioneer Dr Kitaw Ejigu.

Similarly, mastery of the latest developments in science and technology are key to Africa's continued progress as a continent. Mr Holmes lists some of the scientists and engineers, from elsewhere in Africa. Dr Isaac Ghebre-Sellassie of Eritrea, received 23 patents relating to the time release, coating, and stabilisation of drugs. He was involved in the creation of 20 new drug products. Some of his patents were assigned to Warner-Lambert from 1986 to 2003. Samuel Ayodele Sangokoya of Nigeria has over fifty patents in the chemical industry. Many of his patents are assigned to Albamarle Corporation in Richmond, Virginia, between 1992 and 2013. Kofi Afolabi Makinwa of Ghana has over 50 patents for inventions used in computers. Many of his patents were assigned to Phillips Electronics between 1994 and 2007. Among the others to distinguish themselves are botanist Carol V. Ndlovu from South Africa, electric car pioneer Jelani Aliyu from Nigeria, and chemist Clément Kabasele Muamba from Congo, Kinshasa.

As a complex nation with a long history and rich heritage, Ethiopia has distinguished itself in many ways. The Ethiopic writing system has not only underpinned the creation of a splendid and unique literary heritage for our nation of 250,000 old manuscripts, it influenced the formation of two writing scripts in Eastern Europe. Yuri Mikhailovich Kobishanov in the *UNESCO General History of Africa, Volume 2,* shows that the Ethiopic script influenced the creation of the writing scripts of Armenia and Georgia. Readers can see the similarities for themselves. Samples of Ethiopic, Armenian, and Georgian writings can be found on Google Image search. Moreover, the famous Ethiopian manuscript, the *Abba Garima Gospels,* is now believed to date between 330 and 650 AD. Western newspapers, such as London's *The Telegraph,* state that it is generally accepted to be the oldest illuminated Christian manuscript in the world. In addition, the distinguished seventeenth century Ethiopian scholar, Zera Yacob, author of the *Hatata,* is now regarded as a philosopher whose ideas predate those of the European Enlightenment era. This is what Norwegian historian, Dag Herbjørnsrud of the Oslo based SGOKI (the Center for Global and Comparative History of Ideas), wrote about him:

> As the story usually goes, the Enlightenment began with René Descartes's *Discourse on the Method* (1637), continuing on through John Locke, Isaac Newton, David Hume, Voltaire and Kant … By the time that Thomas Paine published *The Age of Reason* in 1794, that era had reached its twilight … But what if this story is wrong? What if the Enlightenment can be found in places and thinkers that we often overlook? Such questions have haunted me since I stumbled upon the work of the 17th-century Ethiopian philosopher Zera Yacob (1599-1692).

He concluded:

> Yacob remained in the cave as a hermit, visiting only the nearby market to get food. In the cave, he developed his new, rationalist philosophy. He believed in the supremacy of reason, and that all humans - male and female - are created equal. He argued against slavery, critiqued all established religions and doctrines, and combined these views with a personal belief in a theistic Creator, reasoning that the world's order makes that the most rational option. In short: many of the highest ideals of the later European Enlightenment had been conceived and summarised by one man, working in an Ethiopian cave from 1630 to 1632.

A *National Geographic* article entitled *Reclaiming the Ancient Manuscripts of Timbuktu* mentioned that some scholars believe that 700,000 manuscripts, some dating to the twelfth century, have survived in

1.
2.
3.
4.
5.
6.
7.

Figure 2. The First Sura of the Koran written in Vai.

the West African city of Timbuktu. They also say the manuscripts 'covered an array of subjects: astronomy, medicine, mathematics, chemistry,' etcetera. The article mentioned other data that is little known today but well worth repeating:

> Beginning in the 12th century, Timbuktu was becoming one of the great centers of learning in the Islamic world. Scholars and students travel[l]ed from as far away as Cairo, Baghdad, and elsewhere in Persia to study from the noted manuscripts found in Timbuktu. Respected scholars who taught in Timbuktu were referred to as ambassadors of peace throughout North Africa.

The Arabic script was used by the literati of Ancient Ghana, Mali, Songhai, the Ashanti Empire, and the Hausa Confederation. Arabic was the main language of learning occupying a similar place in West Africa to that held by Latin in Europe. Many West Africans also used the Arabic letters to write their own languages - this is called Ajami. Ajami manuscripts were written in Songhai, Wolof, Hausa, Fulfulde, Kanuri and Tamasheq. Other West Africans wrote in scripts with characters of a more pictographic nature. In the early days of the Kingdom of Benin, a 'rude' pictographic script was used. In the regions of Sierra Leone and Liberia, the Vai script was used. This was a wholly alphabetic script and was used in the nineteenth century. In addition, the Bamoun Kingdom, now in today's Cameroon, has 7,000 surviving manuscripts in their own script.

But what do we know about the early scientific and technological heritage of Ethiopia? What do we know about the early scientific and technological heritage of indigenous Africans elsewhere in Africa?

This book, *Ancient Science and Technology from Ethiopia and the rest of Africa,* shows that indigenous Africans made respectable contributions that advanced and enriched the metallurgical, mathematical, astronomical, medical, and architectural heritage of all humanity. It is a heritage that we should all be proud of. We should also build on this heritage. However, the ignorance that many of us have about our technological heritage has meant we over rely on non-African technologies and outside expertise by default. We must invest in getting this African heritage taught in schools, universities, and other institutions in Ethiopia and elsewhere in Africa.

His Excellency, Mr Hailemariam Desalegn
former Prime Minister of Ethiopia

PART ONE

ANCIENT SCIENCE AND TECHNOLOGY IN AFRICA

6

INTRODUCTION

What did Ethiopia contribute to the development of science and technology? What did the rest of Africa contribute to the development of science and technology? These two questions form the basis of the research in this book. Aimed at Ethiopian audiences, the book presents Ethiopian contributions to metallurgy, mathematics, astronomy, medicine and surgery, and architecture. It also introduces to Ethiopian audiences the contributions that other indigenous Africans have made to these same areas.

For Ethiopian readers, the book will introduce a scientific and technological heritage that you did not think you had. It will also introduce a scientific and technological heritage from other parts of Africa that you were unaware of. For some non-Ethiopian readers, virtually ALL of this heritage may be new to you. The point of this is to bring a pan African pride in the scientific and technological heritage of Africa that should be taught in every African university and institution whether in Ethiopia or elsewhere.

We show that Africans made great advances in metallurgy. From the invention of mining to the prospecting for metals, to the development of advanced smelting techniques, Africans have a technological heritage to be proud of in bronze, iron, steel, gold, and silver. Did you know that the Tanzania region produced the finest steel anywhere in the world before the year 1850? In the case of Ethiopia, exquisite metal artifacts have been manufactured over the last 2500 years: tools, weapons, monograms, coins, crosses, and crowns.

In mathematics, Africans made great advances. From the invention of numbers to most of the high school maths that we do today, Africans have a mathematical heritage to be proud of: arithmetic, algebra, geometry, fractals, base 10, base 20, etcetera. Did you know that a former Mayor of Timbuktu in Mali arranged for a sixteenth century Timbuktu mathematical manuscript to be translated and sent to France to check the level? The algebraic problems were found to be at the same intellectual level as what was taught in the second year of a French maths degree. In the case of Ethiopia, there are calendrical manuscripts dating from the 4th century AD. The mathematical content of these manuscripts uses algebra, modulo arithmetic, base 2, base 60, and complex fractions.

Africans made great advances in astronomy. From the invention of the lunar calendar, we were the first to devise the notion of time. Africans accurately observe the sun, the moon, and the stars to devise notions of the hour, noon, the solar calendar, etcetera. We also oriented religious monuments to these celestial bodies. In the case of Ethiopia, there were calendrical manuscripts that were used to calculate the times of the religious festivals of the year. Some manuscripts mention solar eclipses in 1241 AD, 1528 and 1727. One manuscript mentions a lunar eclipse in 1620.

In medicine and surgery, Africans made great advances. These advances were so important that it was an enslaved African called Onesimus that introduced the procedure of smallpox inoculation, the predecessor of vaccination, into North America in the early 1700s. The African intellectual heritage includes detailed anatomical knowledge, a wide pharmacopeia, the techniques to successfully perform Caesarion sections, health management regimes, eye cataract surgery, and the control of epidemics. In the case of Ethiopia, there are medical manuscripts dating from the 18th century as well as a wide range of medical and health practices, such as sweating and vapour baths, some of which are still relevant.

Finally, Africa has an interesting architectural heritage of temples, churches, mosques, castles, and town houses. This is perhaps, the least well known of all of Africa's technological developments. But, again, it is a heritage that all Africans can be proud of. For instance, did you know that a mediaeval palace in the Tanzanian city of Kilwa had an indoor swimming pool? Did you know that it was standard practise in mediaeval Mali for town houses in the cities of Timbuktu and Djenné to have indoor toilets on the second floor? Ethiopia, of course, has an impressive architectural legacy of temples, obelisks, churches, and castles from Yeha, Axum, Lalibela, and Gondar.

Where in Africa?

The scientific and technological heritage of Ancient Egypt represents some of the oldest evidence in Africa. The Ancient Egyptians were the pre-Arab indigenes of North and East Africa. These indigenes were as Black and African as other Africans. For instance, mummy skin research shows the

Figure 3. Map of African States (1325 BC 1850 AD). Originally published by Professor W. E. B. DuBois in *The World and Africa*. It was a pioneering and laudable attempt to show the old African states at their point of greatest political expansion. Subsequent research has, however, improved upon this data. Moreover, Mellistine is now more usually called Mali, Bornu-Kanem is usually called Kanem-Borno, Ethiopia is Kush, Abyssinia is Axum, and Zeng (i.e. Zanj) is the Swahili Confederation.

Ancient Egyptians were black complexioned. Professor Cheikh Anta Diop, a Senegalese scholar, conducted research on mummy skin. He took skin samples from mummies discovered by nineteenth century archaeologist Auguste Mariette. He presented the research at a 1974 United Nations event known as The Cairo Symposium. The report says: "They all revealed … the presence of a considerable quantity of melanin."

Similarly, skeletal research shows the Ancient Egyptians had a lanky body shape. Anthropologists can tell populations that evolved in a tropical climate from those that evolved in a cold climate. Africans evolved in a tropical climate. They evolved long arms and legs compared to their overall height. Europeans and Far East Asians evolved in a cold climate. They evolved short arms and legs compared to their overall height. The Ancient Egyptians had a tropically adapted body shape. An article in the *Journal of Human Biology* says: "It is shown that the limbs of the pharaohs, like those of other Ancient Egyptians had negroid characteristics".

Just how old is Ancient Egypt? This is another controversial question. The following table presents the chronological ideas of various authorities and show a great divergence of opinion. Only the chronologies of Champollion-Figeac, Petrie in 1906, MacNaughton, Pochan, and the present author, bear any resemblance to the Egyptian record as preserved by Manetho. This is the timeline that we will stick to in this book.

	DYNASTIES (Dates BC)			
	I	VI	XII	XVIII
Manetho (3rd century BC)	5717	4426	3440	1674
Wilkinson (1836)	2320			1575
Champollion-Figeac (1839)	5867	4426	3703	1822
Lepsius (1858)	3892	2744	2380	1591
Brugsch (1877)	4400	3300	2466	1700
Meyer (1887)	3180	2530	2130	1530
Breasted (1906)	3400	2625	2000	1580
Petrie (1906)	5510	4206	3459	1580
Petrie (1929)	4553	3282	2586	1587
MacNaughton (1932)	5776	4360	3389	1709
Pochan (1971)	5619	4326	3336	1595
Brunson & Rashidi (1989)	3200	2345	1991	1560
Rohl (1998)	2789	2224	1800	1193
Chinweizu (1999)	4443	3162	1994	1788
Author (2006)	5660	4402	3405	1709

This book also deals with the scientific and technological contributions from the West African superstates of Ancient Ghana, Mediaeval Mali, and the Songhai Empire. These empires at the height of their power were centred around the modern Mali region but expanded into the modern territories of Senegal, Gambia, Guinea, Niger, and Northern Nigeria. We also look at the contributions made by the states near to the West African coast including Nok, Igbo-Ukwu, Ife and Benin. These civilisations were in the Nigeria region of today. We also include heritage from Kongo, mostly in modern Angola, and the Ashanti Empire, mostly in modern Ghana. We have also included evidence from more inland including the Kuba and Shongo cultures located towards Central Africa.

This book also deals with the scientific and technological contributions from East and Southern Africa. As well as having a focus on Ethiopia, we also consider the contributions made by the peoples of Ancient Kush and Mediaeval Nubia, located in modern Sudan. We also consider the Swahili Confederation stretching along the East African coast from Somalia, through Kenya and Tanzania, down to Mozambique, the Kingdom of Banyoro (in Uganda), the Empire of Munhumutapa (centred on Great Zimbabwe), and the Zulu Empire (further south).

Finally, in producing this work, we would like to thank Mr Tsegaye Didana of TCD Consulting. A man of great vision, his encouragement got this project across the 'finish line.' We also greatly appreciate the contribution and support of Ambassador Teferi Melesse Desta and His Excellency, Mr Hailemariam Desalegn. The vision that these three eminent gentlemen share will ensure that the light of Ethiopia's legacy will shine in future generations.

Robin Walker & John Matthews

CHAPTER 1: METALLURGY

Ancient Egypt

Professor Charles Finch, the great African American scholar of African antiquities, informs us that the Egyptians were working copper in prehistoric times suggesting dates such as 7500 to 6500 BC. Archaeologists have found copper beads, pins, bracelets, chisels, rings, harpoon heads, needles, and tweezers. By the Fourth Dynasty period, bronze artefacts (i.e., copper combined with 4 to 15% tin) have been recovered. The Egyptians were working gold in pre-dynastic times. Archaeologists found gold beads, a golden ring, a gold cylinder seal, vases covered in golden foil, and knives covered in golden foil. Some objects were of gold alloyed to copper or silver. The Egyptians worked iron as early as pre-dynastic times. However, the oldest known significant piece of iron is a portion of a tool found lodged between joints of the masonry of the Great Pyramid of Giza. Finally, the Egyptians were working steel (i.e., iron combined with up to 2% carbon) by 1200 BC. Two knife blades were found made of low carbon steel of 0.7%.

The West African Coastal States

Some of the earliest metallurgical evidence in West Africa includes a group of iron and copper tools excavated in Senegal dated at 2800 BC and iron smelting in Nok (ancient Nigeria) by 2000 BC. At the Nok sites, blast furnaces and tuyeres were found. Tuyeres are pipes used to conduct air and thus raise temperatures in the metal smelting process.

Metallurgy reached a high point in ninth century AD Eastern Nigeria at a civilisation archaeologists call Igbo-Ukwu. Here, astounding evidence of leaded bronze art and craft were recovered. Leaded bronze is an alloy of copper, tin, lead, and silver worked together. The splendid craft pieces were made using the six-stage lost wax technique.

The lost wax technique involves (i) making a rough clay model of the artefact to be made, (ii) placing a layer of bees wax over the model with all the fine and intricate details, perhaps keeping the wax 3 mm thick, (iii)

Figure 4. Superb vessel in the shape of a seashell from Igbo-Ukwu, ninth or tenth century AD. Leaded bronze. Length 20.6 cm.

place a second layer of clay over the bees wax, (iv) place everything into a kiln and fire it knowing that the melting point of wax is lower than the melting point of clay - the molten wax runs out leaving a 3 mm gap, (v) pour molten metal(s) into the mould replacing the molten wax, and (vi) wait for the molten metal to cool and harden into shape followed by removing the layers of clay. Incidentally, this is the same technique used today to make car parts.

The court art of the Yoruba Kingdom of Ife (eleventh to fifteenth century AD) and the Empire of Benin (sixteenth and seventeenth century) is amongst the very best in the world. Like at Igbo-Ukwu, these kingdoms used the lost wax technique to make the Ife and Benin Bronzes. Art historians prefer the term 'bronzes', but strictly speaking many of the Ife and Benin masterpieces were actually of brass, zinc brass or copper. Copper is a particularly difficult metal to flow through a mould, thus these pieces are not only artistic masterpieces but also technological masterworks.

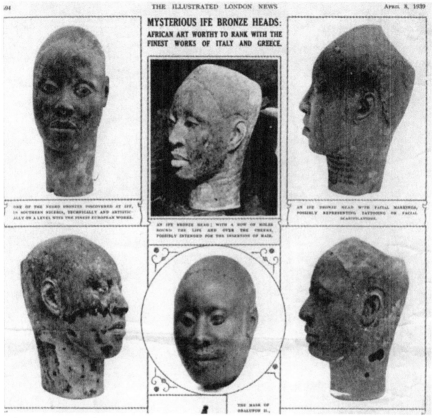

Figure 5. Page from *The Illustrated London News* (8 April 1939) reporting on 'Mysterious Ife Bronze Heads: African art worthy to rank with the finest works of Italy and Greece.' These metal masterpieces date from the eleventh to the fifteenth centuries.

One of these pieces from the fourteenth century shows a soldier wearing chainmail. Songhai records mention helmets, gauntlets and body armour. *On the Obligations of Princes,* a fifteenth century Hausa text, mentions body armour. Chainmail was also used by soldiers in Benin, the Central Saharan Empire of Kanem-Borno and also Sudan on the Upper Nile.

The Yoruba Kingdom of Old Oyo produced iron and steel using very complex technologies that were as advanced as the steel produced on the East African coast of the early mediaeval period. Many writers are now conceding that these East African techniques were the most sophisticated in the world before the middle of the nineteenth century. Clearly the techniques used in Old Oyo were equally sophisticated.

Iron was worked extensively in the Kongo and the Ndongo and Matamba (i.e. in modern Angola) regions in the fifteenth century onwards. The craft of the blacksmith accorded high status to its members. However, linguists working with the Kongolese and other Bantu languages have traced many words to do with metallurgy in their languages back to perhaps 3000 BC. If the words existed back then, then the metallurgical practices must also have existed as well! Whichever be the case, Kongolese metallurgists were well aware of the problems posed by working with lead and had preventative and curative means of combating lead poisoning.

Gold was panned, mined and intricately worked in the Akan and later the Ashanti region of today's Ghana. Giving some idea of the scale of the gold working, one scholar reported that 15 shiploads of local gold were seized by the Portuguese in 1502. The Akan and Ashanti pieces were exquisite works of art and ornamentation. They made bracelets, necklaces, gold decorated weaponry and gold decorated sandals.

The West African Superstates

Gold mining in the Ancient Ghana region (now today's Mauritania and Mali) dates back to the fourth century AD. Gold (and sometimes silver) was used to make swords, shields, bracelets, bells and was turned into thread to embroider cloth. By the twelfth century, gold was minted into coins. The Moors introduced this coinage into Europe that century, which started a trend for gold coins. Mints were established in Northern Spain in the thirteenth century, then Northern Europe in the fourteenth century. One particularly fine piece of Ghanaian gold work is the famous Rao Pectoral found in a twelfth or thirteenth century burial (figure 13).

In Mali, the successor empire, court musicians had instruments covered in gold and silver. The Hall of Audience in Niani, a fourteenth century architectural wonder, had windows with gold and silver frames. In Songhai, the successor empire, the royalty used utensils all covered in gold. The total amount of gold mined to the year 1500 was very conservatively estimated at $35 billion at 1998 gold prices reflecting the combined output of Ancient Ghana, Mali and Songhai. The empires of Ghana, Mali and Songhai had huge golden nuggets and other golden artefacts. Leo Africanus, a sixteenth century visitor, reports that one such golden piece weighed 1300 lbs and was in the possession of the Emperor of Songhai.

As late as 1790, Senegalese gold and silversmiths were still supreme. They produced finer gold and silver work than anyone in Europe at the time. A witness at a British Government Select Committee on the Slave Trade testified to this effect on 29 April 1790.

Kush (i.e., mostly in modern Sudan)

Archaeologists have found copper smelters at Buhen in northern Nubia. These smelters date back to the end of the Old Kingdom Period. According to Professor Finch, tuyères were placed through holes in the smelters where bellows were attached. By fanning the air, the smelters could reach temperatures of over 1,083°C, the temperature needed to melt copper.

Bronze is an alloy of copper and tin. The addition of 4 to 15% of tin greatly improves the strength and hardness of the metal. In Kerma, the inhabitants produced bronze implements of exceptionally fine quality. As late as the Dynasty XXV period, when Kush ruled Egypt, the Kushites were still making high-quality bronze implements. Bronze artefacts continued to be made throughout the Meroitic era which takes us up to 350 AD.

The great archaeologist, Sir Flinders Petrie, found a cache of 23 tools from the Dynasty XXV period. Consisting of punches, chisels, files, rasps, adzes, etcetera, five of these pieces were analysed by scholars. They found that two of the five were actually made of low carbon steel. The carbon content amounted to no more than 0.1 or 0.2%. However, this was sufficient to produce a metal three times harder than iron.

Iron implements were discovered in Kushite graves dating back to around 750 BC. Archaeologists found an iron bangle, tweezers, an arrowhead, a hook, a blade, an axe head, an unsocketed knife, and an adze. The city of Meroë was of course the centre of the Kushite iron industry. Archaeologists used to call Meroë 'the Birmingham of Africa' due to its massive iron industry. However, some African historians have suggested that Birmingham, England, should instead be called 'the Meroë of Europe.'

Gold and silver were among the royal metals of Kush. Gold was so commonplace that silver was often considered even more valuable than gold. Numerous examples of exquisite golden ornaments have come down to us including jewellery, inlay, and sculpture.

Perhaps the most celebrated example was discovered in 1834 by an Italian grave robber. Destroying the Pyramid of Kentake Amanishakheto, the grave robber discovered superlative examples of Kushite gold work known as the Treasures of Amanishakheto. Other golden pieces recovered from Kush include ornate amulets, wadjet eyes, knives, decorated cylinder

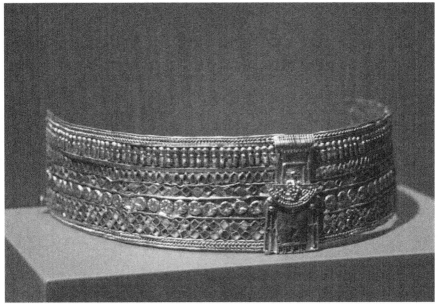

Figure 6. Armlet from the Treasures of Amanishakheto. Gold and fused glass inlays. Height 3 cm. Width of each piece 9.2 cm. (Photo: Sven-Steffen Arndt.)

sheaths, tweezers, gold flower necklaces and earrings. The temples at Meroë and Musawarat had walls and statues covered with gold leaf.

East Africa

Archaeologists have found iron smelters in East Africa going back before 600 BC. A number of examples were found in Rwanda, Burundi, Uganda, the Sudan, Kenya, Congo and Tanzania. Iron itself is derived from haematite ore. In certain parts of East Africa, surface haematite is relatively plentiful on certain hillsides. Metallurgists typically preheated the ore in very hot fires for approximately half an hour thus easing the separation of the iron from the ore before completing the main smelt. However, smelting required large quantities of charcoal which in practice meant that perhaps 15 medium-sized trees could end up being consumed in the process!

The early East Africans used two main types of smelters. One type was a large bowl set into the ground. The second type had a tall shaft perhaps 10 feet above ground. The shaft was often made of a special clay which contained quartz, mica and feldspar making the structure fireproof. It is likely that the tall furnace was used for the initial smelt and the bowl smelter was used to refine the metal produced from the tall furnace.

Archaeologists found a number of steel furnaces in the Lake Victoria region that dated back to about 500 AD. This finding is important because it indicated that certain peoples in what is now northern Tanzania (such as the Haya) were producing high carbon steel that was technically unsurpassed by anybody until the middle of the 19th century. The archaeologists reconstructed the furnaces to show how they worked. They discovered that the ancient metallurgists worked at around 1450°C. They also found that in some parts of the combustion zone, they reached temperatures as high as 1820°C. This was the highest temperature achieved in a blast furnace anywhere before the middle of the 19th century. This is significant as Professor Charles Finch explains:

> These astonishingly high temperatures explain a unique characteristic of Haya iron: contrary to bloom iron found throughout the world that forms by the sintering of fine solid particles, Haya iron forms by the precipitation of large crystals from the ore. The molten slag then undergoes a "carbon boil"--similar to the process in modern blast furnaces--resulting in a formation of two products pure iron and steel. This is an extraordinarily efficient way of producing iron since it requires less fuel than the standard Iron Age smelting techniques. As Nikolaas Van Der Merwe has pointed out, this methodology represents a significant technical innovation in steel manufacture that seems to have been unique to Africa. There are at least four places where crystalline steel was produced: Tanzania (Haya), Nigeria (Oyo), Ethiopia (Lake Tana), and Ghana, all presumably by similar methods. Thus, the induced draft furnace with a tall shaft plus preheating of bellows-driven air are two unique African inventions. The laborious processes of carburization, quenching, tempering, and hammering so characteristic of steel-making in other parts of the world seem to have been bypassed in a technical tour de force among those African peoples mastering the "Haya technique".

The Tanzanian steel was traded by the Swahili in the Middle Ages to make the famous Damascus blades. The historian, Al Idrissi, in the *Book of Roger* (1153) makes special mention of what he calls 'superior iron'. This is a reference to the early Tanzanian high-quality steel.

Southern Africa

Archaeologists beginning in 1902 began the rediscovery of Southern African gold mining in and around the Great Zimbabwe region. They found thousands of gold mines dug to an astonishing depth of 150 feet. The archaeologists estimated that the southern Africans dug 43,250,000 tons of ore. According to Professor Finch, this produces 700 tons of pure gold which equals $7.5 billion at 1998 gold prices.

Figure 7. Old iron smelting furnace from the Zimbabwe region. From J. Theodore Bent, *The Ruined Cities of Mashonaland, 3rd Edition,* UK, Longmans, Green, and Co., 1902.

One historian wrote: 'The bygone miners must have been industrious beyond belief, since they worked in rock so obdurate that the same sort of reef is nowadays blasted with dynamite, and yet they removed many million tons of ore. It is a practical testimony to their skill that the modern engineers follow to this day the lines of their ancient workings.'

Gold was used to make ornaments, jewellery and plate objects. All the goldsmith's art was practiced there including gold wire drawing, beating gold into thin sheets, plating iron and bronze with gold, and burnishing. Golden thread was woven into cloth and gold chain links were produced. Gold was used to cover furniture to make figurine statuary, arrowheads and battleaxes.

Also in 1902, archaeologists found fifty pounds of iron hoes, a huge quantity of coiled wire of bronze, copper, and iron, some of which were twisted into bracelets. Also found were numerous copper ingots, copper jewellery, iron gongs and stone moulds for copper ingots. More recent archaeology has found abundant evidence of iron and copper mining shafts and furnaces dating from the eighth century AD.

Ethiopia

Artefacts from the Yeha period have survived. The height of this culture was about 600 or 500 BC. Their metallurgists produced bronze vessels, lamps, weapons, and tools. Amongst these were axes, chisels, daggers, spears, and sickles. They also made an unusual body of objects that were used as personal seals or monograms. Between 8 and 11 centimetres across, the designs combine open work geometrical shapes, animal designs, and characters of the Proto Ethiopic alphabet. These objects presumably encoded the owners name and were stamped on pottery.

In the Empire of Axum, bronze was used alongside gold and silver to make coins. These were minted between the 3rd and the 8th centuries and names 24 rulers. They also made colossal sculptures of bronze some of which were more than 15 feet in height. Equally skilled in gold, the Axumites casted large golden statues. What is remarkable, however, is the extent to which the Axumites entered the Steel Age. As Professor Finch points out, virtually all of their weapons were made of steel.

Cross shaped pendants of great beauty and a wide variety of designs were probably made in the early days of Ethiopian Christianity. These artefacts were probably of bronze. And typical of metal objects made elsewhere in Africa, they were manufactured using the lost wax technique. David Buxton, an authority on Ethiopian antiquities, speculates that the surviving examples in silver date from the fifteenth century and possibly the nineteenth century. Another body of crosses are the much larger priest crosses. These are depicted in 15th century Ethiopian manuscripts but, of course, may be older. Then we have the processional crosses, made of copper, bronze, or iron. David Buxton states that these crosses date back to the Agau period (980-1270 AD). However, Belai Giday, an indigenous scholar, suggests they may date back to the Axum period. Whichever be the case, their elaborate designs using fractal shapes has attracted the attention of the mathematician, Professor Ron Eglash.

Exquisite royal crowns have survived from the 17th century. Made of gold, these works are intricate and elaborate.

Coinage is the most distinguished Ethiopian use of metallurgy. In ancient times, Ethiopia was one of the few kingdoms which issued coins in gold. The only contemporary states which issued gold coins at the time were the Kushan Kingdom in northern India, the Persian Empire, and the Roman Empire. The coins were of gold, silver, and bronze. Other metals were sometimes used but these were often overlaid with gold on key symbols

Figure 8. Coin of the Axumite ruler Ousanas. (Photo: Classical Numismatic Group, Inc.)

such as the crown, the cross and the royal head. The coins are important for other reasons. The names of several unknown kings are preserved on their coinage. Therefore, the coins are crucial for comprehending Axumite chronology.

The first Ethiopian king to issue coins was Endubis (c.270-300 AD). Some claim that he was the first ancient African king to issue his own coins. His coins became the archetype to be followed by his successors. The coins' main image is of the king himself. Above his head are the divine symbols of the moon disc and crescent. The coin shows him wearing an Axumite tiara. The legend in Greek gives the title "King of the Axumites". Moreover, his gold coin has ears of barley or wheat which framed the royal portrait. Although ears of wheat as central heraldic motifs have been used by other kingdoms, they do not appear in the form of those found on Axumite coinage.

The Christian cross replaced the moon disc and crescent following the conversion of King Ezana (320-c.360). Ezana was the first monarch to embrace Christianity. Axumite kings were probably the first Christian rulers to show the cross on their coins. The kings are dressed in fringe robes, necklaces, armlets, and bracelets. They hold a sword and a spear, however during Christian times they are holding a cross. The king was represented on both sides of the gold coin. This double representation is almost unique in world coinage and demonstrates the importance that the royal image had in the Axumite kingdom. On silver and bronze coins, an image of the king wearing a headcloth is shown on the obverse whilst a variety of designs are shown on the reverse.

King Aphilas experimented with different designs. One of his gold coins had the feathered white crown of the ancient Egyptian and Sudanese deity Osiris. Another gold coin was equivalent to a fraction of a Roman aureus (coin worth 25 silver denarii). His silver coin displays his portrait on both sides but also had the disc and crescent symbolism. Perhaps this king followed pre-Christian religious traditions. King Aphilas' most common silver coin is gilded. The obverse shows the king's head and shoulders. The reverse shows a similar image of the king but set in a circle. Considering the size of the coins, gilding on its reverse demonstrates the exceptional technological skills of the die cutters.

King Wazeba succeeded King Aphilas and changed the language used on his gold coins. The legends on his coins were written in Ge'ez as well as Greek. Several coins have been unearthed that indicate that Wazeba may have ruled with Ousanas. It could be argued that Wazeba requested that a colleague or son reigned with him. This was the system which was later employed by Roman Emperor Diocletian with the tetrarchy. The coins show Wazeba on the obverse and Ousanas on the reverse.

King MHDYS used Ge'ez on one of his bronze coins; the legend on the coin reads "By this cross you will conquer", which is a legend from the vision from Constantine the Great. The rulers declared messages to their subjects through the legends on coins. Some coins issued by King Ezana show the cross in the centre encompassed by the words "May this please the people", "Christ is with us" or "Joy and peace to the people".

Kaleb has more gold coin issues than any other Axumite king. This may be because he led a famous campaign to the Yemen, against the Jewish King Yusuf Asar Yathor because of his attacks against Christians. This military campaign may have required the production of gold coins to pay his troops. Kaleb had a coin inscribed with the motto 'Theou Eukharistia' (i.e., By the grace of God). The other type of gold coin displays the legend "Uios Thezana" which means 'Son of Tazena'. The silver coin of Kaleb shows the royal bust with the Axumite Tiara. In Ge'ez is inscribed "May this please the city".

CHAPTER 2: MATHEMATICS

Ancient Egypt

The Ancient Egyptians made important contributions to the origin and evolution of mathematics. The Ancient Greek scientist, Aristotle, recognised this and wrote the following in his work *Metaphysics*: 'And thus Egypt was the cradle of the mathematical arts.'

Four Ancient Egyptian mathematical documents survive today and have been the subject of considerable research by modern scholars - the *Rhind Papyrus,* the *Berlin Papyrus,* the *Moscow Papyrus* and the *Kahun Papyrus.* These papyri indicate that a large proportion of high school mathematics was created by the Ancient Egyptians.

The Egyptians had a decimal system with special symbols for the numbers 1, 10, 100, 1,000, 10,000, 100,000 and 1,000,000. They had fractions, but these are always given as 1/2, 2/3, 1/3, 1/4, 1/5, 1/6, etcetera. With the exception of 2/3, all the other fractions were expressed as one over two, one over three, and so on. These are called unit fractions. If the Ancient Egyptians wanted to express 3/4, they would write 1/2 + 1/4. In a similar vein, if they wanted to express 2/5, they would write 1/3 + 1/15. They were adept at handling fractions. Problem 33 of the *Rhind Papyrus,* for example, required the student to calculate 16 + 1/56 + 1/679 + 1/776 + 10 + 2/3 + 1/84 + 1/1358 + 1/4074 + 1/1164 + 8 + 1/112 + 1/1358 + 1/1552 + 2 + 1/4 + 1/28 + 1/392 + 1/4753 + 1/5432 = 37!

The *Rhind Mathematical Papyrus* was probably a Middle Kingdom Period (i.e. Eleventh or Twelfth Dynasty) student's copy book that contains 87 mathematical problems and their solutions. Belonging to an individual student called Ahmose, the text is a record of what he was taught. Beginning with arithmetic and number theory, the student worked with formulae in the areas of algebra, geometry, trigonometry and π. For example, problem 24 asks. 'A quantity plus its seventh becomes 19. What is the quantity?' It required the student to solve for one unknown called *'aha'* meaning 'heap'. If problem 24 was written today *'aha'* would be transcribed as 'x' and the question would look like this: $x + x/7 = 19$. What is x?

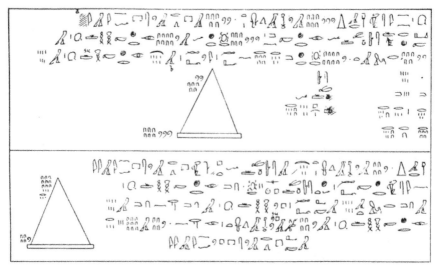

Figure 9. Sketch of problems 56 and 57 from the *Rhind Mathematical Papyrus*. These are the oldest known examples of trigonometry depicted in a mathematical document.

Problem 41 asks: 'Find the volume of a cylindrical granary of diameter 9 and height 10.'

Problem 50 addresses the area of a circle. The question asks: 'Example of a round field of diameter 9 *khet*; what is the area?' The suggested formula and method gave an approximation for π as 256/81 which is 3.1605 to 4 decimal places. This is closer to the real figure of π (i.e. 3.14159 etcetera) than the figure 3 used by the Ancient Babylonian mathematicians.

Problem 51 asks: 'A demonstration of the calculation of a triangular plane. If asked: A triangle 10 rods high, 4 at its base; what's its area?'

Problem 52 asks: '[T]rapezium of 20 *khet,* with a large base of 6 *khet* and a small base of 4 *khet*. What is its surface?'

These four problems (41, 50, 51, 52) thus addresses the volume of a cylinder, the area of a circle, the area of a triangle, and the area of a trapezium. What else is in the papyrus?

Problem 56 asks: 'If a pyramid is 250 cubits high and the side of its base 360 cubits long, what is its *seked?*' This is a trigonometry problem requiring the student to calculate the *seked* (or cotangent) of the slope of the pyramid.

Problem 79 asks: 'Inventory of an estate: Houses: 7   Cats: 49   Mice: 343   Barley seeds: 2401   Bushels: 16807.' According to Professor Théophile Obenga, a leading authority on Ancient Egyptian texts, this means:

'Suppose that on an estate of 7 houses, each house had 7 cats, each cat killed 7 mice, each mouse ate 7 barley seeds, and each barley seed would have yielded 7 bushels; how many bushels would that make all told?' In mediaeval times the Italian mathematician Fibonacci wrote: 'Seven old women went to Rome: each woman had seven mules; each mule carried seven sacks: each sack contained seven loaves; and with each loaf were seven knives; each knife was put up in seven sheaths.' This is a seven step geometric progression of 7 x 7 x 7 x 7 x 7 = 16807. If written today, the question would have said: 'Find the sum of 5 terms of the Geometric Progression whose first term is 7 and whose common ratio is 7.'

The *Moscow Mathematical Papyrus* contains 25 mathematical problems of which Problems 10 and 14 are widely regarded as high points in the evolution of Ancient Egyptian mathematics.

Problem 10 asks: 'Method of calculating a basket. If it is said to thee, a basket with an opening of 4 1/2 in its containing, Let me know its surface.' The term basket means 'hemisphere.' Thus, the problem concerns the difficult problem of calculating the surface area of a hemisphere. The formula the scribe used was S = 2d x (8/9) x (8/9) x d, where S is the surface area and d is the diameter, which is almost equivalent to $S = 2\pi r^2$, the way the formula is presented today. The only difference is that the Egyptians reckoned π to be 256/81 or 3.1605.

Problem 14 asks: 'Method of calculating a truncated pyramid. If it is said to thee, a truncated pyramid of 6 *ellen* in height, of 4 *ellen* of the base, by 2 of the top.' The solution used the formula of $V = h/3 (a^2 + ab + b^2)$ where V is the volume, a is the base, b is the length of the top, and h is the height. Historians of science and mathematics claim that this method has not been improved on in 4000 years!

The *Berlin Mathematical Papyrus* contains formulae for solving for two unknowns. Problem 1 asks: 'How to divide 100 into two parts such that the square root of one part is 3/4 of the square root of the other part.' In modern algebraic expressions, it looks like this: $x^2 + y^2 = 100$, where y = 3/4x. Other scholars present it like this: $x^2 + y^2 = 100$, where 4y - 3x = 0. Either way, everyone agrees that this problem requires calculating two unknowns, x and y, from two simultaneous equations.

The *Kahun Papyrus* Plate VIII has a mathematical problem on it that has baffled scholars. Professor Cheikh Anta Diop, the brilliant Senegalese scholar, speculates that it is dealing with the volume of a sphere with a hemisphere of 8 units in diameter. Other writers holding a different opinion think it concerns the volume of a cylindrical silo of 8 units in diameter and 12 units in height.

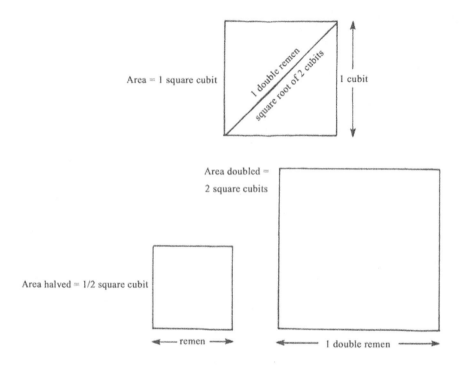

Figure 10. As Professor Beatrice Lumpkin points out with these squares, there is a demonstrable relationship between an Egyptian royal cubit and another Egyptian measurement called a double remen. A double remen is equal to the square root of 2 royal cubits. This is particularly interesting because the square root of 2 equals 1.4142 etcetera. It is an irrational number. Many scholars see this as convincing evidence that the Ancient Egyptians were familiar with the concept of irrational numbers.

The Ancient Egyptians made other contributions to mathematics that shall be summarised briefly. They pioneered the 3, 4, 5 triangle which is the basis of the so-called 'Pythagorean Theorem.' They used this triangle to accurately calculate right angles. That the Egyptians knew this triangle, the following excerpt by Plutarch, the great Greco-Roman scholar, is most edifying: 'The Egyptians appeared to have figured out the world in the form of the most beautiful of triangles … This triangle, the most beautiful of triangles, has its vertical side composed of three, its base of four, and its hypotenuse of five parts, and the square of the latter is equal to the sum of the squares of the two sides.'

Finally, there is evidence of a more controversial and contested nature that the Old Kingdom Egyptians knew about irrational numbers. Many scholars credit the Egyptians with the knowledge of the square root of 2 (which is 1.4142), a more detailed understanding of pi or π (3.14), and also phi or ϕ (1.618). This data was built into the proportions of the Great Pyramid of Giza.

Yoruba

Just imagine having to calculate (200 x 3) - (20 x 4) + 5 before being able to say 'five hundred and twenty five.' According to mathematician, Professor Claudia Zaslavsky, an American specialist on African mathematics, you 'must be a mathematician' to use the Yoruba number system. For this reason, learning Yoruba numerals have a pedagogical value in Nigeria and among some of the African Americans. Educators see the value in teaching this system to pupils since it gets them to use arithmetic in just being able to express the numbers. This system has been in use for hundreds of years and may well date back to the glory days of the Kingdom of Ife.

The Yorubas evolved a complicated numerical system that often involves subtraction and multiplication to express a single number. The Yoruba phrase for three hundred and fifteen is *orin* (which means 20 x 4) *din nirinwo* (from 400) *odin marun* (less 5), which, in mathematical symbols, becomes 400 - (20 x 4) - 5 = 315. The English equivalent 'three hundred and fifteen' is simply (3 x 100) + 15 = 315, making use of multiplication and addition, but no use of subtraction. Many centuries ago, however, when Roman numerals were used across Europe, subtraction was also used. The Roman IV, for example, is 5 - 1, and IX is 10 - 1.

The Yorubas had separate terms for one to ten: i.e. *ookan, eeji, eeta, eerin, aarun, eefa, eeje, eejo, eesan* and *eewaa*. From ten to fourteen, the Yorubas use addition. Their phrase for eleven, for example is *ookan laa*, which is 10 + 1 = 11. The other numbers mean 10 + 2, 10 + 3 and 10 + 4. However, for fifteen, they say *eedogun*, which derives from *arun* (five) *din ogun* (from twenty) or 20 - 5 = 15. The other numbers from sixteen to nineteen are 20 - 4, 20 - 3, 20 - 2, and 20 - 1. Between twenty and thirty, there is a similar pattern - addition is used from twenty-one to twenty-four and subtraction is used from twenty-five to twenty-nine. For example, twenty-two becomes 20 + 2 and twenty-six becomes 30 - 4.

The Yorubas count in base 20, in contrast to what we use today - base 10. Consequently twenty, and numbers that are multiples of twenty, are important in their system. The word for twenty is *ogun*. The word for forty is *ogoji*, which is derived from *ogun* (twenty) and *eeji* (two). Sixty is *ogota*, derived from *ogun* and *eeta* (three), and eighty (*ogorin*) comes from *ogun* and *eerin* (four). In mathematical symbols, 40 = 20 x 2, 60 = 20 x 3 and 80 = 20 x 4. They have special names for important base 20 numbers, such as *igba* (200) and *irinwo* (400), just as the English have special names for important base 10 numbers such as 100 (hundred).

For numbers fifty, seventy and ninety, subtraction is used. The term for fifty is *aadota*. It comes from *ogota,* which, as we have seen, means 20 x 3, and *laa* which is ten, but in this context means minus ten. Fifty is therefore (20 x 3) - 10, seventy is (20 x 4) - 10 and ninety is (20 x 5) - 10. The Yoruba terms for numbers forty-five to forty-nine are complicated, as are sixty-five to sixty-nine and eighty-five to eighty-nine. For example, 46 = (20 x 3) - 10 - 4, 67 = (20 x 4) - 10 - 3 and 88 = (20 x 5) - 10 - 2.

The Yoruba number system had terms for unit fractions 1/2, 1/3, 1/4 and 1/5, etcetera. The Yoruba divination system called the *Odu Ifa* had phrases for 4 raised to the power of 2 (meaning 4 x 4 = 16), 4 raised to the power of 3 (i.e. 4 x 4 x 4 = 64) and, 4 raised to the power of 4 (i.e. 4 x 4 x 4 x 4 = 256). The Yorubas also had an indigenous notion of infinity and they had a word for million (*egbeeberun*).

The West African Superstates

How is it possible to arrange numbers into a table using each number only once so that each row, each column, and the two diagonals all add up to the same number? This question had intrigued Chinese scholars for thousands of years. However, West African scholars were also interested in this puzzle.

Archaeologists working in the Malian city of Djenné revealed some interesting information. Karen E. Lange explains:

> In the base of a wall from about A.D. 1400 they found fragments of a type of bowl the Djennenké [i.e., people of Djenné] still place in foundations for protection. One fragment carried magical grids or squares; another was inscribed with a benediction in Arabic; the third had the date 512 - or, adjusting from the Islamic calendar, A.D. 1118.

Thus, the people of Djenné were familiar with magic squares at least as early as 1400 or even as early as 1118 AD. But what are magic squares?

A magic square is a mathematical recreation or game. It is constructed by arranging numbers into a table where each row, each column, and the two diagonals, all add up to the same number called the magic constant. A Hausa scholar from the University of Katsina, Ibn Muhammad, published

32	14	38	20	44	26	1
48	23	5	29	11	42	17
8	39	21	45	27	2	33
24	6	30	12	36	18	49
40	15	46	28	3	34	9
7	31	13	37	19	43	25
16	47	22	4	35	10	41

Figure 11. A seven-order magic square with 175 as the magic constant. All the rows, columns and the two diagonals add up to 175. Notice also that the distance on the square from '1' to '2' shows the same relationship as the knight's move in chess. Similarly, the distance from '2' to '3' also requires a knight's move. This is also true of '3' to '4', '5' to '6', etcetera.

a book in 1732 with examples in it. Professor Claudia Zaslavsky made a special study of this manuscript, originally called: *A Treatise on the magical use of the letters of the alphabet.*

Ibn Muhammad worked with three order squares (i.e., 3 x 3 = 9 squares in total), five order squares (i.e., 5 x 5 = 25 squares in total) right up to eleven order squares (i.e., 11 x 11 = 121 squares in total). He also demonstrated how a given magic square can be reflected about the vertical axis, the horizontal axis, and about the two diagonals. Moreover, he showed how a given square can be rotated through 90 degrees, 180 degrees and 270 degrees.

Professor Claudia Zaslavsky, mentioned earlier, shows that a magic square of odd number n (3, 5, 7, etc.), consists of a square array of numbers from 1 to n^2, then the magic constant will be equal to $n(n^2 + 1)/2$. For example, if we try to construct a seven order magic square (7 x 7 = 49), then $n = 7$. This means that the numbers used will be 1 to 7^2 (= 49) and the magic constant will be $7(7^2 + 1) \div 2 = 175$.

Commenting on this, Professor Charles Finch, an authority on African science history, noted that this shows 'the "algebraic" quality of magic squares and why a sound knowledge of number theory is important in their creation.' This raises the question: Did West Africans only get as far as algebra?

A *New Scientist* article by Curtis Abraham had plenty to say on the practise of mathematics at Timbuktu which answers this question:

[T]he Muslim scholars of Timbuktu would ... have had particular reasons to be
interested in astronomy. First is the requirement for Muslims to pray, and to
orient their mosques in the direction of Mecca. To achieve this, they needed to
develop algorithms and instruments to determine the exact position of both
Mecca and Timbuktu. There was also the need to determine exact times for
prayers at sunrise, noon, afternoon, sunset and evening. The scholars found
ancient Greek methods of doing this very cumbersome, the researchers say, but
Muslim astronomers devised easier solutions by inventing the cosine, tangent,
cotangent, secant and cosecant functions of trigonometry.

So, Timbuktu scholars were familiar with cosines, tangents, cotangents,
secants and cosecant functions. Moreover, mathematics was one of the
liberal arts taught at the Songhai universities. The scholars, Hunwick and
Boye, state that Timbuktu scholars purchased and copied manuscripts on
geometry and calculus. Professor Henry Louis Gates, the famous African
American academic, drew attention to a surviving manuscript in a
Timbuktu library on mathematical accounting. What academic level did the
Timbuktu mathematicians reach? A former Mayor of Timbuktu, Ali Ould
Sidi, arranged for a sixteenth century Timbuktu mathematical manuscript
taught at the Timbuktu University of Sankore to be translated and sent to
France to check the level. The algebraic problems were found to be at the
same intellectual level as what was taught in the second year of a French
maths degree.

Benin and Congo

It may seem the height of disrespect to compare the old and exquisite Benin
Bronzes or the fabulous Congolese Textiles to wallpaper, but there is a
connection. Wallpaper, despite its apparent blandness, is actually a treasure
trove of applied mathematical techniques. Typical wallpaper designs are
based on a single idea or motif that is repeated across the paper using two
geometric operations, translation and reflection.

Translation is where a motif is repeated by moving it in a straight line
from its original position to position one, two, three, four, etcetera.
Reflection is where a motif is repeated as if it were a mirror image of the
original. Reflection can take place along a vertical axis, making the left
hand side of the original motif, the right hand side of the reflected motif. It
can also take place along a horizontal axis, making the bottom of the
original motif the top of the reflected motif.

There are 24 different combinations of translation and/or reflection
(including rotating the motif by 60 degrees, 90 degrees, 120 degrees, 180

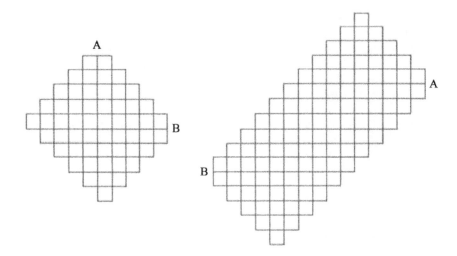

Figure 12. In order to draw these networks, one must start at the entry points A or B.

degrees or 360 degrees) that can be used to cover a wall. The proof that there were only 24 such techniques allegedly came from a Russian scholar called Federov in 1891. An analysis of Islamic art, however, proved that the Islamic world had long made use of all 24 techniques. This raised the question of whether this knowledge existed in West and Central African arts and crafts.

Dr D. W. Crowe and Professor Zaslavsky made independent studies of the Benin Bronzes of the Nigeria region and the Bakuba Textiles from the Congo region. The Benin masterpieces were mostly from the sixteenth century and the Congolese crafts were mostly from the eighteenth century. Dr Crowe concluded that 17 of the 24 possible mathematical techniques appeared in the Benin Bronzes, and 'at least' 19 of the 24 techniques appeared in the Bakuba Textiles.

Other uses of geometry are demonstrated by a game traditionally played by Shongo children in the Congo region. According to mathematician Professor Beatrice Lumpkin, the game involved drawing complex networks with a continuous line or path, without taking one's pen or pencil off the page and without tracing the same line twice. A European mathematician, Leonhard Euler, developed solutions to this problem in 1735. He also established a new branch of topology called network analysis. However, according to Professor Lumpkin, it is likely that the Shongo games are much older than the time of Euler.

Figure 13. The Rao Pectoral, twelfth or thirteenth century AD. 22 carat gold, 18 cm in diameter.

Professor Paulus Gerdes, a leading authority on African mathematics, reveals that traditional African know-how often demonstrates sophisticated geometrical knowledge. He demonstrates this by using examples of African wall decorations, rolled up mats, woven knots, woven pyramids, square mats, plaited mats, and plaited strips. For more information readers are referred to his *Geometry from Africa* (US, The Mathematical Association of America, 1999). To give an example, artisans from Mozambique traditionally used hexagonal weaving techniques to make hats, handbags, transportation baskets and fish traps. If the strips used for the craft making were of equal width, they were traditionally plaited at 60 degrees to each other. Other angles would have been used if the strips were of different widths. The 60 degree angles meant that the finished craft pieces contained equilateral triangles, rhombi, trapeziums, and regular hexagons.

Finally, West Africans (and Africans elsewhere) made practical use of fractal geometry. Fractals are characterised by repeated geometric patterns over ever diminishing scales. The Rao Pectoral was a magnificent golden artefact buried with a vassal prince of Ancient Ghana from the twelfth or thirteenth century AD. This pectoral uses the circle over and over at different scales, offering a pleasing aesthetic. Professor Ron Eglash, an expert on fractals, shows that Africans used fractal geometry in architectural ornamentation, architectural plans, and even in hair braiding. Moreover, there is even a clear relationships between African use of fractals and the binary code.

Ethiopia

A few years ago, BBC 4 presented an interesting short film about multiplication in Ethiopia as part of a series about mathematics and number. Entitled *Go Forth and Multiply,* the film explained the millennia old system of multiplication used in Ethiopia by its traders and merchants. One of the products that the traders sold was coffee. Interestingly, coffee had its origins in Ethiopia.

If an Ethiopian trader wanted to multiply 11 and 15, he would put the numbers into two columns. He would place the 11 in one column and he would place the 15 in the other column.

In the first column he would continually halve the number ignoring the fractions. Thus 11 halved is 5 (i.e. ignoring the fractions), halved again is 2, and halved again is 1. In the other column he would double the numbers.

Thus 15 doubled is 30, doubled again is 60, and doubled again is 120. The two columns might look like this:

Halving column	Doubling column
11	15
5	30
2	60
1	120

There is a rule that one must IGNORE any even number(s) in the halving column AND the corresponding number(s) in the doubling column.

Consequently, we shall ignore the 2 and the 60. Our table now looks like this.

Halving column	Doubling column
11	15
5	30
1	120

Finally we add up the numbers in the doubling column to produce our answer which is $15 + 30 + 120 = 165$.

The narrator commented that: "It seems unbelievable that a system can ignore fractions, even throw away parts of the calculation and still come up with the right answer."

The underlying principle of this system is doubling which, at its core, is base 2 arithmetic. The narrator explained the significance of this: "It's a system that seems completely foreign to Western eyes but in fact we use it thousands of times a day because it's this system that powers today's computers."

When is Easter? How do we calculate it? Ethiopia possesses interesting chronological ideas preserved in its mediaeval manuscripts. Professor Otto Neugebauer studied these manuscripts dating mostly from the fourteenth to the nineteenth centuries and wrote two books: *Ethiopic Astronomy and Computus* and *Chronography in Ethiopic Sources.*

As well as a hollow month of 29 days and a full month of 30 days, Neugebauer found indigenous Ethiopic terms in the manuscripts for zero, the hour, a solar cycle of 28 years, a jubilee of 49 years and a 'seal' of 76 years.

Neugebauer found that the Ethiopians had a lunar calendar. The Ethiopians alternated hollow months of 29 days with full months of 30 days. This produced a lunar year of 354 days. They calculated this as $(29 + 30) \times 6 = 354$. Once every four years, they would add an extra day to the lunar year making 355 days.

The Ethiopians also had an Enoch year of 364 days. Coming from the astronomical information in one of their holy books, the *Book of Enoch,* they calculated this as four equal seasons of 91 days each i.e. $91 \times 4 = 364$. 91 days is also equal to 13 weeks of 7 days since $13 \times 7 = 91$.

There was also an Alexandrian year which averaged 365 1/4 days. For three out of every four years they would have a 365 day year named after the three evangelists in the Bible, Matthew, Mark and Luke. The year consisted of 12 months of 30 days each plus five extra days i.e. $(12 \times 30) + 5 = 365$. On each fourth year, named after the evangelist John, they would add a sixth extra day giving a total of 366 days. This is similar to the leap year calculation that we use today.

The difference between the Alexandrian year and the Lunar year for three out of four years was 11 days i.e. $365 - 354 = 11$ days. For the years named after the evangelist John, the difference was also 11 days i.e. $366 - 355 = 11$ days.

Most importantly, Neugebauer found that Ethiopian scholars and historians used a 532 year cycle as their basis for calculating time. What is the basis of the 532 year cycle?

When the Ethiopians compared the Alexandrian year to the Lunar year, they found that the lunar year was shorter by 11 days i.e. 365 - 354 = 11. After two years it was 22 days shorter i.e. 11 x 2. After three years it was 33 days shorter i.e. 11 x 3. At this point the Ethiopians would add another lunar month of 30 days. Over a period of 19 Alexandrian years, they discovered the need to add a total of 7 lunar months. Since there are 12 lunar months in a year, there are 228 lunar months in a 19 year period i.e. 19 x 12 = 228. Since it was necessary to add 7 extra lunar months, there were 235 lunar months in every 19 Alexandrian years. This 19 year cycle became a key part of Ethiopian calculations.

The Ethiopians had a seven day week. Sunday is called the Christian Sabbath, the names for Monday to Friday are based on the Ethiopian numbers 2 to 6, and Saturday is called the First Sabbath. With each passing year the days of the week at each date change. After a period of 7 years, the days of the week and the dates coincide.

Thus the 532 year cycle embodies the 19 year cycle, the 4 year cycles of the years of the evangelists, and the 7 day week. 532 is the lowest common multiple of 19, 4 and 7 since 19 x 4 x 7 = 532. It also embodies another Ethiopian unit of time called a 'seal' which is of 76 years. A seal is composed of 4 lots of 19 year cycles i.e. 4 x 19 = 76. There are 7 seals in 532 years since 7 x 76 = 532.

How did the Ethiopians calculate Easter? They made extensive use of modulo arithmetic.

Modulo arithmetic is where there is a limit on the highest number that can be calculated from a procedure. Once that number has been reached, we return to one and complete the calculation. For instance, the highest number on an analogue clock is 12. After this the next number is 1. So if a question required the calculation of 11 pm + 3 hours, the answer would be 2 am and NOT 14 pm! Mathematicians would pose this same question as: What is 11 + 3 modulo 12? This tells us that 12 is the highest possible number. The next number after 12 is 1, then 2, etcetera. If the question was posed as: What is 11 + 23 modulo 12? The answer cannot be 34 since the highest possible number is 12. The quickest way to arrive at an answer is to divide 34 by 12 and the answer is the remainder. 34 divided by 12 is 2, the remainder is 10. Thus the answer to 11 + 23 modulo 12 is 10. When writing the formulae, it is customary to shorten modulo to 'mod'.

In explaining these ideas, I shall use two symbols that the reader may be unfamilar with (i) $\equiv$ and (ii) $\leq$. The first symbol means 'equivalent to'. It is similar to, but not quite the same as, 'equals'. Therefore '$c \equiv$ W mod 19' means that c is equivalent to W where 19 is the highest possible number. The second symbol means 'less than or equal to'. Therefore 'I 15 $\leq m \leq$ II 13' tells us that the lowest possible figure for m is month I day 15 and the highest possible figure for m is month II day 13.

The Ethiopians reckoned time in big blocks of data called Eras. The oldest era was the Era of the World. Beginning 5492 BC this represented the beginnings of creation from Ethiopia's Biblical perspective. Beginning 5036 BC was the Era of Bizan, named after an Ethiopian monastery. Beginning 8 AD was the Era of Incarnation. Beginning 284 AD was the Era of Martyrs. Finally beginning 360 AD was the Era of Grace. Ethiopian scholars believed that the Second Coming of Christ was to be in Year 7000 of the Era of the World. One of the manuscripts suggested that this means that human existence would total 2,548,000 days (i.e. 364 days x 7,000 years). Another manuscript suggested that this meant a total of 2,556,750 days (i.e. 365 1/4 x 7,000).

The Ethiopians saw time as repeated cycles of 532 years which they tabulated in 28 tables of 19 years each (i.e. 28 x 19 = 532). The ultimate aim of these tables was to help calculate the day and date of Easter each year since this is a moveable lunar and solar festival. In 2014, for example, Easter Sunday was celebrated on 20 April. In 2015 it will be celebrated on 5 April.

W	c	e	m	t	f
1	1	0	30	3	13
2	2	11	19	4	2
3	3	22	8	5	25
4	4	3	27	6	9
5	5	14	16	1	1
6	6	25	5	2	21
7	7	6	24	3	6
8	8	17	13	4	25
9	9	28	2	6	17
10	10	9	21	7	2
11	11	20	10	1	22
12	12	1	29	2	13
13	13	12	18	4	5
14	14	23	7	5	18

15	15	4	26	6	10
16	16	15	15	7	1
17	17	26	4	2	21
18	18	7	23	3	6
19	19	18	12	4	26

Figure 14. This is taken from the first of the 28 19-year tables showing information for years 1 to 19. W means years of the world, *c* means cycle number of years, *e* means epact, *m* means matqe'e, *t* means tentyon and *f* means fasika. What these terms mean and how they are calculated will be explained over the next few pages.

In calculating the day and date of Easter for any one of the 532 years, the Ethiopian scholars made a number of calculations using a number of interrelated algebraic formulae. We shall illustrate this by calculating Easter for Year 472 of their system.

First, they calculated a parameter that Professor Neugebauer calls 'cycle number of years, from 1 to 19.' Neugebauer symbolised it with a *c*. This parameter was calculated for any of the 532 years, symbolised by W meaning 'Years of the World', modulo 19. Thus 19 was the highest possible number from the calculation. The next number after this was 1, then 2, etcetera. Since Year 472 is much higher than 19, we need to divide it by 19 and the remainder is the answer. Thus:

$c \equiv W \qquad \mod 19$
$472/19 = 24$ remainder 16
Thus $c \equiv 16 \mod 19$

Second, they calculated a parameter called the Epact. Symbolised in Neugebauer's analysis by an *e,* the Epact measured the running total of differences between the 354 day lunar year and the 365 day solar year. After one year, the difference was 11 days. After two years, the difference was 22 days. After three years, the Ethiopians would add an extra lunar month. Consequently, the difference in the third year was reduced from 33 days, to just 3 days. To calculate the Epact for any given year, they used a formula equivalent to the one given below:

$e \equiv (c - 1) \times 11 \qquad \mod 19$
$(16 - 1) \times 11 = 165 \equiv 15 \qquad \mod 19$
Thus $e \equiv 15 \mod 19$

Third, they used the Epact to calculate a third parameter called the Matqe'e. Symbolised by Neugebauer using an m, it was the date of the Jewish New Years Day. Ethiopia is home to a very ancient Black Jewish community. The earliest date that Matqe'e could fall on was day 15 of the first Ethiopian month (i.e. I). The latest date that it could fall on was day 13 of the second Ethiopian month (i.e. II). It was calculated by subtracting the Epact from 30. Thus:

$m = 30 - e$ where I $15 \leq m \leq$ II 13
$m = 30 - 15 = $ I 15 (i.e. month I, day 15)

Fourth, they used the Matqe'e to calculate Passover or p. The earliest date that Passover could fall on was day 25 of the seventh Ethiopian month (i.e. VII). The latest date that it could fall on was day 23 of the eighth Ethiopian month (i.e. VIII). It was calculated by adding 190 to the Matqe'e, modulo 30. Thus:

$p = m + 190$ where VII $25 \leq p \leq$ VIII 23
$p = 15 + 190 = 205 \equiv 25$ mod 30
Thus $p = $ VII 25 (i.e. month VII, day 25)

Fifth, they calculated a parameter called the Tentyon or t. This was the day of the week on which the Ethiopian New Years Day fell (not to be confused with the Jewish New Years Day). It was the first day of the first month, (i.e. I 1) but there was a formula they used to work out which day of the week this was. By tradition, the Ethiopian scholars *who compiled these manuscripts* considered Wednesday to be the first day of the week, Thursday became the second day, etcetera. To calculate the Tentyon, they used a formula equivalent to the one given below:

$t \equiv W - 1 + 1/4 (W - 1)$ mod 7
$472 - 1 + 1/4 (472 - 1) = 588.75$
588.75 rounded up becomes 589 or $\equiv 1$ mod 7
t = Day 1 = Wednesday

In the next two steps, the Ethiopian scholars calculated the day of the week for Matqe'e (Jewish New Years Day) and the day of the week for Passover. Professor Neugebauer shows that these calculations did not require any complex formulae. They relied on simple arithmetic. For instance, if the first day of the first Ethiopian month (i.e. I 1) was a Wednesday, then the Matqe'e being on I 15 is also going to fall on a Wednesday. If the Passover was 190 days later and 189 days is a multiple of 7, then the 190th day will be a Thursday.

For the final calculation of Easter Sunday or f (meaning Fasika), the Ethiopians relied on simple arithmetic. Easter Sunday was always celebrated as the Sunday after Passover. Since Passover was on Thursday VII 25, then Easter Sunday was three days later. The earliest date that Easter Sunday could fall on was day 26 of the seventh Ethiopian month. The latest date that it could fall on was day 30 of the eighth Ethiopian month. Thus:

$f =$ VII 25 + 3 = VII 28   where VII 26 $\leq f \leq$ VIII 30

The Ethiopians used other formulae to calculate other festivals of the year. Chief among these were the Beginning of Fast (or bf) and the Ninevah festival (or n). They calculated these by formulae equivalent to the ones given below:

$bf = f - 55$ mod 30   where VI 1 $\leq bf \leq$ VII 5
$n = bf - 14$ mod 30

W	c	t	f
457	1	3	17
458	2	4	2
459	3	5	22
460	4	7	13
461	5	1	28
462	6	2	18
463	7	3	10
464	8	5	29
465	9	6	14
466	10	7	6
467	11	1	26
468	12	3	10
469	13	4	2
470	14	5	22
471	15	6	7
472	16	1	28
473	17	2	18
474	18	3	10
475	19	4	23

Figure 15. This is taken from one of the 28 19-year tables showing information for years 457 to 475. W means years of the world, c means cycle number of years, t means tentyon and f means fasika.

Using the example of Year 472, the Beginning of Fast was on VI 3 and the Ninevah festival was on V 19.

Using the Ninevah festival, the Ethiopians calculated other Christian festivals. Among these were Mount Olive (which was $n + 41$), Hosanna (which was $n + 62$), Synod ($n + 93$), Ascension ($n + 108$), Pentecost ($n + 118$), Prayer of Salvation ($n + 121$), and Fast of the Apostles ($n + 126$). Both the actual formulae and the modulo 30 versions appear in the Ethiopian manuscripts.

Base 60

Some manuscripts discuss sexagesimal or base 60 fractions of the day. Others contain a concept called *kekros*. What does this strange term mean? Professor Neugebauer mentions diagrams and texts from Ethiopian manuscripts that describe the changing illumination of the waxing or waning moon. The manuscripts present this as a linear sequence which varies between 4 *kekros* and 60 *kekros* in 15 steps of 4 *kekros* each. Thus each *kekros* represents 1/60 of the diameter of the illuminated fraction of the lunar disk. Other manuscripts show that 4 *kekros* means 48 minutes and 60 *kekros* means 12 hours. Thus 1 *kekros* means 12 minutes in this instance. A different manuscript shows that 15 *kekros* means 1 hour and 360 *kekros* means 24 hours. Bringing this evidence together, Professor Neugebauer concludes that *kekros* refers to 1/60.

One particularly impressive use of base 60 appears in an Amharic manuscript. The manuscript gave the mean value of a synodic month as 29:31,50,7,57,30d. How should this be interpreted? This shows that the value was $29 + 31/60 + 50/60^2 + 7/60^3 + 57/60^4 + 30/60^5$ days in length. This is clearly a complex calculation.

CHAPTER 3: ASTRONOMY

Ancient Egypt

Astronomy is the science of mapping the heavenly bodies including the sun, the moon, the stars and the other planets. Throughout the ages, humans have used astronomy to tell the time, devise calendars, orientate buildings and as a guide to travel.

The Ancient Egyptians pioneered the use of the sundial, the clepsydra (water clock) and the merkhet (i.e. a device using a straight edge and a plumb line to measure stars). The Ancient Egyptians also wrote texts on astronomy that were famous in Greek and Roman times but unfortunately have not survived into our times. One document was called *On the Disposition of Fixed Stars and Stellar Phenomena.* Another text was entitled *On the Disposition of the Sun, Moon and Five planets.* Yet another document was called *On the Syzygies and Phases of the Sun and Moon.* By the way, syzygies are the lining up of 3 or more celestial bodies such as an eclipse. A fourth text was called *On Risings.*

Duncan MacNaughton, author of the erudite *A Scheme of Egyptian Chronology,* reproduced an image of the astronomical ceiling in the Tomb of Senenmut, a contemporary of Hatshepsut (seventeenth century BC). The ceiling has twelve months of the year depicted. He also reproduced a picture of the heavens from the Ramesseum (fourteenth century BC), again with the twelve months of the year depicted.

The Ancient Egyptians invented the 365 day solar calendar based on astronomical observation. They also created the concept of the month and the zodiac based on the grouping of stars. They grouped at least 43 stellar constellations.

Their most important contribution to astronomy, however, was their creation of the Sothiac or Sothic Cycle which is superior to the concept of the leap year that we use today. The Sothiac Cycle is based on the fact that the earth spins 365¼ times each time it orbits the sun. Since it is impractical to have the concept of ¼ of a day, we moderns have adopted the practice of having a leap year of 366 days once every four years to 'correct' for this problem.

Figure 16. Water clock from Karnak used for estimating the time over the twelve hours of night.

The Ancient Egyptians had a cleverer way of dealing with this. They ran a civil calendar of 365 days but also ran a more accurate calendar of 365¼ days at the same time. After one year, the two calendars would disagree by ¼ of a day. After two years, the two calendars would disagree by ½ a day. After three years, the two calendars would disagree by ¾ of a day. After four years, the two calendars would disagree by a whole day. We can therefore calculate that after eight years, the two calendars would disagree by two days. After twelve years, the two calendars would disagree by three days, etcetera. Keeping these calculations going, after 1460 years of 365¼ days, the two calendars would disagree by a whole year and thus the first day of the year on one calendar would be the first day of the year on the second calendar! The 1460 year period is called the Sothiac Cycle.

A Roman scholar called Censorinus stated that the two Egyptian calendars met up with each other in 139 AD. This meant that the two calendars met up with each other 1460 years earlier i.e. 1321 BC. The two calendars met up with each other 1460 years before this, i.e. 2781 BC. Finally, the two calendars met up 1460 years before this, i.e. 4241 BC. Thus the Egyptian astronomers did not need to use the concept of a leap year.

Concerning the origin of the zodiac, there was a lively intellectual battle between Sir E. A. Wallis Budge and Dr Albert Churchward in the early twentieth century over whether the Ancient Egyptians or the Ancient Greeks invented it. The argument centred on the zodiac painted on the ceiling of the Temple of Hathor at Denderah. The temple was known to have been very ancient and may have dated to the time of Fourth Dynasty

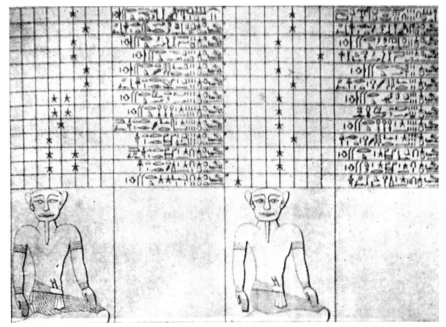

Figure 17. Detail from a star calendar from the time of Rameses VI of the Twentieth Dynasty which, according to Duncan MacNaugton, represents 'a star calendar for each of the twelve hours of night on the 1st and 16th of each month of the year.'

Pharaoh Khufu (4824-4761 BC). However, the temple standing there today was renovated in the time of the Greek rulers of Egypt, the Ptolemaic Dynasty. So the controversy is this: Did the Greeks add the zodiac to the renovated building or was it there in Pre-Greek times possibly as early as the time of Khufu?

A careful examination of the Denderah Zodiac shows that the image of Cancer is not a crab, as one might expect, but it is actually Khepera the dung beetle. The significance is this. Europe does not have dung beetles, and thus Europeans changed the dung beetle into a crab. Therefore, had the Greeks invented the zodiac they would have placed a crab there instead of a dung beetle. We conclude therefore that Dr Churchward was correct. There was, however, Greek influence on this zodiac. A few of the animals are depicted looking to the side and are shown with dramatic poses that differ from the stiff formalism of Ancient Egyptian art. All the other animals show the stiff formalism of Ancient Egyptian art. It is thus easy to distinguish Egyptian originals from the Greek influences. This all combines to suggest that the Denderah Zodiac was indigenous in origin.

Figure 18. Sketch of the Denderah Zodiac from a controversial Egyptian Temple built by the Egyptians but renovated by the Greeks. Who was responsible for the zodiac?

The Roman geographer Strabo wrote a comment in his *Geography* which was most edifying on this subject: 'The Greeks lacked knowledge of the real length of the year and several similar facts until translations of the memoirs of Egyptian priests into the Greek language spread these ideas among astronomers, who have continued to this day to rely heavily on this same source.'

The zodiac divides the year into twelve houses or constellations. This is one of the ways that the concept of the twelve months of the year came about. If the Ancient Greeks lacked indigenous knowledge of the true length of the year they could not have divided it into the twelve months.

The Ancient Egyptians pioneered the heliocentric theory i.e. the idea that the earth and the planets orbit the sun (says Sir Isaac Newton). They knew

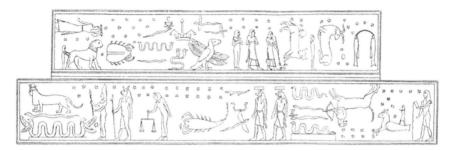

Figure 19. Zodiac from the Temple of Esneh. Duncan MacNaughton feels that this 'may be a late version of an earlier zodiac.' In support of this idea, he points out that: 'The zodiac also has the peculiarity that before the sign Virgo a Sphinx is inserted, a lion with the head of a woman, surely a symbol of the transition from Virgo to Leo. This suggests that the colossal Sphinx carved out of rock near the pyramids of Cheops and Kephren belongs to the same period. It is usually attributed to Kephren and therefore if from internal evidence the date of this zodiac can be fixed we obtain a probable date for Kephren.' If MacNaughton is correct about this, then the original on which it was based would go back to the Fourth Dynasty i.e. to the time of Khehpren better known as Khafra, the son of Khufu mentioned earlier.

of the planets Mercury, Venus, Mars, Saturn and Jupiter. The year is, of course, the orbit of the Earth around the Sun. The month is, of course, the orbit of the Moon around the Earth. They calculated and predicted lunar eclipses. This is where the earth comes between the sun and the moon, which causes the earth to throw its shadow over the moon. Moreover, the Egyptians invented the hour. This is the length of time it takes the moon to move its own diameter relative to the sun.

The earth wobbles as it spins, just like a spinning top. This produces two measurable effects as far as we earthlings are concerned, the precession of the equinoxes and the changes in the circumpolar constellations.

The precession of the equinoxes can be explained as the very slow, cyclic changes in the coordinates of the fixed stars that takes place over a time period of approximately 25,900 years. This enormous period of time is called a Great Year (of 25,900 years) and can be divided into smaller units called an Age or a Great Month (of 2,160 years). Twelve Great Months is equal to one Great Year (i.e. 2160 x 12 = 25,920). The Ancient Egyptians discovered this when they noticed that when the sun rose on the morning of the Spring Equinox, the longest day of the year, there was a particular zodiacal constellation on the Eastern horizon where the sun rose. On each Spring Equinox, they expected to see the same zodiacal constellation. However, after a period of 2160 years, the zodiacal constellation at the Spring Equinox where the sun rose changed to the next zodiacal

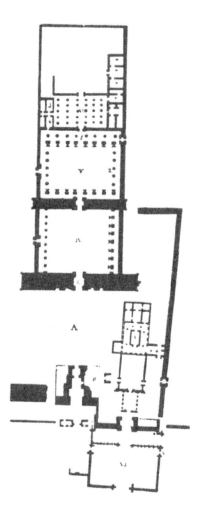

Figure 20. Sir Norman Lockyer suggested that the altered plan of some of the temples, such as this one at Medinet Habu, was a response to the precession of the equinoxes.

constellation. After another period of 2160 years, the Spring Equinox would change to the next zodiacal constellation. It would take a Great Year of approximately 25,900 years to complete the cycle to where the sun would rise on the morning of the Spring Equinox where the first zodiacal constellation would be on the Eastern horizon. This phenomenon is called the precession of the equinoxes because the changes to the zodiacal sign over each Great Month goes backwards (i.e. the precession) to the previous zodiacal sign and not forwards to the next zodiacal sign as one would expect.

Other scholars present this information in other ways. According to George Goodman: 'Our entire solar system with all its planets and moon describes a huge circle around another sun in space, viz., the star Sirius. This movement takes 25,920 years to complete and, during that time, our Sun appears [to us earthlings] to traverse through various constellations or star clusters ... By arbitrarily dividing that huge circle into twelve sections (or houses) they gave to each of them an appropriate sign and name and called the duration of 2,160 years an age. Twelve of these ages constitute one complete turn of our solar system around Sirius.'

Sir Norman Lockyer, the great English astronomer, proved that the Ancient Egyptians knew this by showing that the Egyptians re orientated their temples to keep them in line with shifting stellar phenomena over the thousands of years.

The circumpolar constellations can be described as the constellations that the North Pole of the earth would point to if it was extended into space. It is considered a pole, because these are the constellations that appear to change their positions THE LEAST as the earth turns on its axis. However, changes in the circumpolar constellations take place every 3,700 years. In the period of a Great Year they change seven times (i.e. 3700 x 7 = 25,900).

A number of scholars writing over the last two hundred years believe that the Ancient Egyptians discovered both phenomena; the precession of the equinoxes and the changes in the circumpolar constellations. Some of these writers claim that the Ancient Egyptians began calculating both phenomena beginning 10,858 BC. As an example, Richard Allen wrote: 'Many have maintained that Egypt was the first to give shapes and names to the star-groups; Dupuis, perhaps inspired by Macrobius of our 5th century, tracing the present solar zodiac to that country and placing its date 13,000 years anterior to our era.'

Professor Théophile Obenga, the great Congolese Egyptologist, noticed some interesting scientific ideas hidden in two Ancient Egyptian religious hymns.

Pharaoh Akhenaten of the Eighteenth Egyptian Dynasty wrote *The Great Hymn to Aten*. A passage in the hymn read as follows: 'Living sun disk, you who brought life into being ... trees and grass grows green ... your rays reach deep into the great green sea.' Professor Obenga noticed the link between sunlight giving life and the colour green. He believes that this is an early understanding of the concepts that we moderns would call photosynthesis and chlorophyll.

Stele 826 in the British Museum contains the text of *Hymn to Amen Ra*. A passage from this hymn read as follows: 'In one short day you voyage millions of leagues and hundreds of thousands. Each day is just an instant for you.' Professor Obenga noticed that this is a reference to the vast speed at which light travels. The actual figure is 5 hours from the Sun to Pluto, the farthest planet.

The Dogon

The Dogon are a non-Islamic people in modern Mali. Their knowledge has created quite a stir since the early nineteenth century. They traditionally taught their initiates about the Rings of Saturn, four of the (nine) Moons of Jupiter, the spiral structure of the Milky Way Galaxy, and the desolate surface of the Moon. Dogon knowledge was revealed to the world through the writings of a French initiate into the Dogon system, Marcel Griaule, who wrote up the information in a book called *The Pale Fox.*

How far back do Dogon calculations go? The Dogon have a tradition of choosing a new priest every 60 years at the SIGUI festival. This is where the orbits of Jupiter and Saturn synchronize. Based on the number of changes of priests and other cultural data, most writers date the Dogon knowledge to the early 1200s AD. Thus the Dogon were a part of the histories of the Mediaeval Mali and Songhai Empires. However, linguists point out that the Dogon language, and thus the Dogon culture is very ancient indeed.

The Dogon evolved a 354 day lunar calendar, a 365 day solar calendar, a Sirius calendar which implies (but does not prove) a 365.25 day calendar, and a Venusian agricultural calendar based on the six positions or phases of the planet Venus.

The Dogon have sophisticated ideas based on a star called Sirius 'B.' Sirius 'B' is a star that orbits Sirius. To the unaided eye, it is invisible. The Dogon elders maintain that it is the smallest and densest type of star in our galaxy, an idea confirmed by modern astronomy. The Dogon say that Sirius B orbits Sirius every 50 years, also confirmed by modern astronomy.

Controversially, the Dogon say that Sirius B rotates on its own axis each year and they celebrate this at the BADO celebration. They also say that another companion star, Sirius C, is four times larger than Sirius B. Modern astronomers cannot confirm or deny these propositions and so the jury is still out. Whichever be the case, Professor Finch says: 'it is the Dogon who deserve credit for having discovered Sirius B and the white dwarf as a category of star.'

The Dogon today are a relatively poor and isolated population. This raised the question of: How did the Dogon know any of this advanced

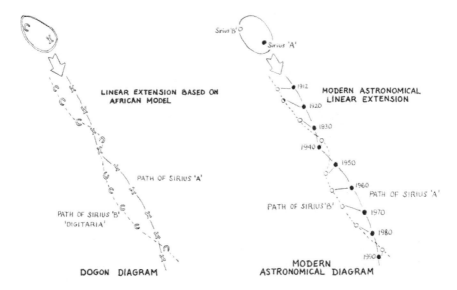

Figure 21. Sketch drawn in the sand by Dogon elders to initiates concerning Sirius A and B compared to the ideas of modern astronomers.

scientific knowledge? Mr Hunter Havelin Adams III, an African American authority on African and African American science history, believes that the Dogon have inherited part of the knowledge acquired from the astronomers and mathematicians at the Mediaeval West African University of Timbuktu. We believe that it could just have easily been the other way round. It could be that the Timbuktu scholars learned their ideas from the Dogon.

Timbuktu

Michael Palin, in his TV series *Sahara,* said the imam of Timbuktu:

> has a collection of scientific texts that clearly show the planets circling the sun. They date back hundreds of years ... Its convincing evidence that the scholars of Timbuktu knew a lot more than their counterparts in Europe. In the fifteenth century in Timbuktu the mathematicians knew about the rotation of the planets, knew about the details of the eclipse, they knew things which we had to wait for 150 almost 200 years to know in Europe when Galileo and Copernicus came up with these same calculations and were given a very hard time for it.

However, not all scholars are agreed with all of this. A *New Scientist* article by Curtis Abraham gave the following information on Timbuktu Astronomy:

While they may have got it wrong about the motion of the planets, the manuscript reveals that the scholars had precise methods for defining the Islamic calendar, including algorithms on how to determine leap years. The algorithms were as accurate as anything mathematicians have today, as Medupe found when he tested them against the modern, computer-based approach. "These people were very knowledgeable about the subject they wrote about," he says. Other manuscripts dating back 600 years include beautifully drawn diagrams of the orbits of planets, which demonstrate the use of complex mathematical calculations. There are also recordings of astronomical events, including a meteor shower in August 1583. Another manuscript discusses the use of an astronomical instrument to determine the direction of Mecca.

What is at issue here between Palin and Abraham is that SOME Timbuktu manuscripts have the EARTH as the centre of the Solar System and not the sun. However, both men are agreed that Timbuktu mathematicians had calculated the orbits of the planets well over a century before Galileo and Copernicus.

Professor Rodney Thebe Medupe, the South African astrophysicist mentioned in the *New Scientist* article, is the leading authority on Timbuktu Astronomy. He wrote the 2009 film documentary *The Ancient Astronomers of Timbuktu.* He illustrated a number of astronomical themes in the documentary using specific Timbuktu manuscripts, such as:

The direction to Mecca - the qibla - for the five daily prayers, using spherical trigonometry and a simpler method using the gnomon.
Calendars - the lunar and solar calendar systems and the difference between various calendars around the world.
A method to calculate leap years.
Sine quadrant - using information from a manuscript the researchers use a quadrant to tell the time by measuring the angle of the Sun.
Information from a manuscript to show how to use the 28 lunar mansions to tell the time at night.
A copy of a manuscript with tables originally written by a renowned medieval Egyptian astronomer with calculations and information on the positions of the planets, moon and stars.

Kush and Christian Nubia

Astronomy has had a long history in early East Africa. Scholars from Greco-Roman antiquity and pioneering Orientalists from the late eighteenth century shared the view that astronomy had its distant origins in 'Ancient Ethiopia' i.e. Nubia or Kush. Unfortunately, not enough archaeological evidence has survived in the Sudan to confirm this. Consequently, we must regard these ideas of the Greco-Roman scholars and the eighteenth-century pioneers as speculative. Intelligent speculation to be sure, but speculative, nonetheless.

African American historian, Professor John G. Jackson, was fully convinced by the eighteenth-century research. He wrote:

> In the study of ancient affairs, folklore and traditions throw an invaluable light on historical records. In Greek mythology we read of the great Ethiopian king, Cepheus, whose fame was so great that he and his family were immortalised in the stars. The Queen Cassiopeia, and his daughter. Princess Andromeda. The star groups of the celestial sphere, which are named after them are called the ROYAL FAMILY - (the constellations: CEPHEUS, CASSIOPEIA and ANDROMEDA.)

Did the Nubians or Kushites really invent astronomy? The voice of history gives us a clue. A book on astrology attributed to Ancient Greek writer Lucian declares that: "The Ethiopians were the first who invented the science of stars, and gave names to the planets, not at random and without meaning, but descriptive of the qualities which they conceived them to possess; and it was from them that this art passed, still in an imperfect state, to the Egyptians".

Pioneering Orientalists shared this view. Count De Volney wrote *The Ruins of Empires,* one of the glories of eighteenth-century literature. De Volney invoked the weighty authority of Charles F. Dupuis, whose three monumental works, *The Origin of Constellations, The Origin of Worship* and *The Chronological Zodiac,* are marvels of meticulous research. Dupuis placed the origin of the Zodiac in Nubia or Kush as far back as 15,000 B.C. Professor John G. Jackson says 'This estimate is not excessive as it might at first appear, since the American astronomer and mathematician, Professor Arthur M. Harding, traces back the origin of the Zodiac to about 26,000 BC.' Count De Volney gives the following glowing description of the scientific achievements of the Ancient Ethiopians, and of how they mapped out the signs of the Zodiac:

> It was, then, on the borders of the upper Nile, among a black race of men, that was organised the complicated system of the worship of stars, considered in relation to the productions of the earth and the labours of agriculture ...Thus the Ethiopian of Thebes named stars of inundation, or Aquarius, those stars under which the Nile began to overflow; stars of the ox or bull; those under which they began to plough, stars of the lion, those under which that animal driven from the desert by thirst, appeared on the banks of the Nile; stars of the sheaf, or of the harvest virgin, those of the reaping season; stars of the lamb, stars of the two kids, those under which these precious animals were brought forth ... Thus the same Ethiopian having observed that the return of the

inundation always corresponded with the rising of a beautiful star which appeared towards the source of the Nile, and seemed to warn the husbandman against the coming waters, he compared this action to that of the animal who, by his barking, gives notice of danger, and he called this star the dog, the barker (Sirius). In the same manner he named the stars of the crab, those where the sun, having arrived at the tropic, retreated by a slow retrograde motion like the crab of Cancer. He named stars of the wild goat, or Capricorn, those where the sun, having reached the highest point in his annuary tract ... imitates the goat, who delights to climb the summit of the rocks. He named the stars of the balance, or Libra, those were the days and nights being equal, seemed in equilibrium, like that instrument; and stars of the scorpion, those where certain periodical winds bring vapors, burning like the venom of the scorpion.

Cepheus is a constellation in the northern sky. In Greek mythology, Cepheus was an Ethiopian (i.e., Nubian or Kushite) king, the husband of Queen Cassiopeia and the father of Princess Andromeda. Cassiopeia foolishly boasted that Andromeda was more beautiful than the Nereids, angering Poseidon. Consequently, the sea god sent a flood and sea monster named Cetus to attack Ethiopia. The King and Queen consulted a wise oracle of Ammon in the Libyan desert. The oracle pronounced that the disaster will not cease until their beautiful daughter Andromeda was offered to the monster. King Cepheus chained his daughter to a rock to be consumed by the sea monster. Whilst Perseus was flying home with the head of Medusa, he noticed Andromeda chained to a rock and was mesmerized by her beauty; he fell in love with her at first sight. Perseus accepted the challenge to slay the sea monster if Andromeda would marry him; Perseus slew the monster with his sword. The Ethiopian king and queen allowed Perseus to become Andromeda's husband. After spending about a year in the court of King Cepheus, Perseus set off for home with his beautiful Ethiopian (i.e., Nubian or Kushite) wife. The name Cassiopeia means Queen of Ethiopia. The Cassiopeia constellation is in the northern sky and remains one of the 88 modern-day constellations.

Moving from intelligent speculation to evidence that can be fully corroborated by archaeology, Professor Finch reports that the Nile Valley Africans engaged in the calculations of lunar eclipses dating from the time when Kush ruled Egypt as Dynasty XXV. Lady Lugard tells us that on the base of one of the Kushite pyramids, a Zodiac was discovered. Professor Diop reports that Lepsius discovered in Meroë the foundation of an astronomical observatory. On the walls of the edifice was found a scene representing people operating an instrument resembling an astrolabe. He also found a series of numerical equations relating to astronomic events which occurred two centuries BC.

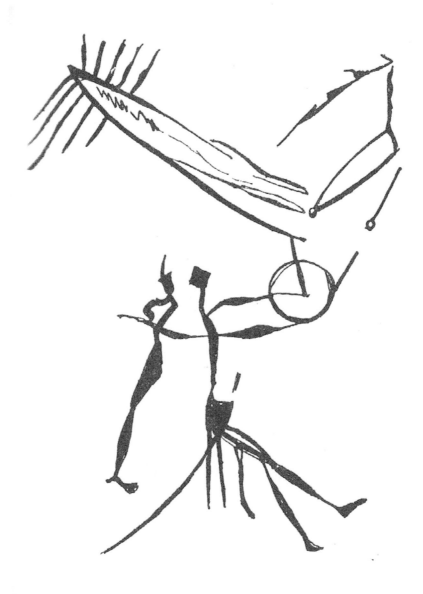

Figure 22. Petroglyph from Meroë showing people operating an astronomical instrument. Is this an astrolabe?

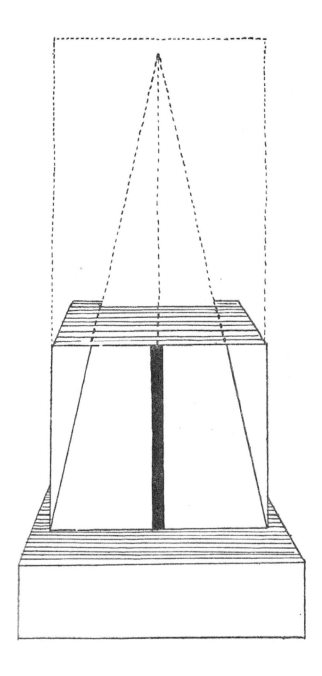

Figure 23. Instrument from Meroë that enabled the tracking of the sun at the meridian.

Another tantalising example comes from a Mediaeval Nubian tombstone. The royal burial inscription from Soba East, capital of the Kingdom of Alwa, reads as follows:

> O God of the spirits and all flesh, Thou who hast rendered death ineffectual and has trodden down Hades, and hast given life to the world, rest the soul of (Thy) servant David, the King, in the bosom of Abraham and Isaac and Jacob, in a place of light, in a place of verdure, in a place of refreshment, whence pain and grief and mourning hath fled ... The years from his birth when he was not a king (were) [..] whereas he was king 16 years 3 months. After the Martyrs 732 he completed (his life) in the month of Hathor the 2nd; Thursday.

The Month of Hathor is a concept associated with the Ancient Egyptians. The fact that this appears on a Mediaeval Nubian tombstone may indicate that the Mediaeval Nubians inherited the Ancient Egyptian calendar. This also suggests that they inherited at least portions of the Ancient Egyptian astronomical lore.

Early Kenya

Other substantial research into East African astronomy came from the pen of two archaeologists working in Kenya in the 1970s who discovered a significant early site. Called Namoratunga II, Lynch and Robbins wrote a paper on it entitled: *Namoratunga: The First Archaeoastronomical Evidence in Sub-Saharan Africa,* 1978. The site was dated at 300 BC and is regarded as evidence of early astronomy in the Lake Turkana region of Kenya.

Nineteen pillars were found at the site. They were at odd angles but were found to have been allied to certain stars. The archaeologists numbered the pillars and suggested that their pillars 1, 5 and 18 were the sighting points. If they were correct in this assertion they concluded that from pillar one, the ancient astronomers were observing Triangulum, the Pleiades, Aldebaran and Bellatrix. From pillar five, the ancient astronomers were observing Aldebaran, Central Orion, Saiph and Sirius. From pillar 18, the ancient astronomers were observing Bellatrix, Central Orion, Saiph and Sirius.

Lynch and Robbins suggested that the ancient astronomers were observing the stars to create an accurate 354 day lunar year divided into 12 months. The idea was that the early astronomers waited for certain stars to line up against certain pillars in conjunction with the new moon. For the first month of the year, they waited for the star Triangulum. For the second

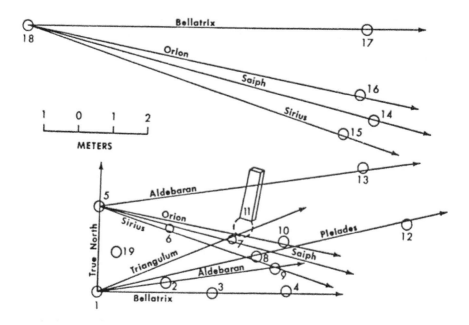

Figure 24. Pillar alignments at Namoratunga II in Kenya. *c.*300 BC.

month it was the Pleiades. For the third month it was Aldebaran, followed by Bellatrix, followed by Central Orion, followed by Saiph, followed by Sirius. For months eight, nine, ten, eleven and twelve, the astronomers observed the star Triangulum, but calculated it against the declining phases of the moon. This lunar calendar was one of the most accurate of the pre-Christian era calendars.

Great Zimbabwe

Concerning Great Zimbabwe, Professors Oliver and Fagan have pointed out that the New Moon ceremonies in May signalled the beginning of their civil calendar. Laurance Doyle, author of an encyclopaedia of the history of science, technology and medicine in the non-Western world has interesting things to say about the astronomical ideas encoded into the building of the Great Zimbabwe.

> [P]reliminary investigations do reveal that the native African peoples that built Great Zimbabwe were aware of the sky and may indeed have marked important astronomical seasonal events. For example, in a preliminary survey, a "chevron" pattern on the southeast corner of the large outer wall is bisected by

the rising position of the Sun on the summer solstice from inside the enclosure, and aligns with what has been called the "altar" as well as an original pillar inside the enclosure. As this large patterning does not appear at any other place on the outer wall it would appear to be a conspicuous candidate for a summer solstice marker built into the Great Enclosure. In addition, a large passageway within the Great Enclosure--about 2 meters in width, 30 or so meters in (curving) length, with 10 meter high brick walls on either side, would allow a limited view of the sky with an angular extent and curvature matching the position and angular extent of the Milky Way overhead on the summer solstice. While the Milky Way was a very important calendrical marker for the Karanga people of this area [who are a part of the Shona] (Sicard 1969, McKosh 1979) this observation too must be confirmed with further research. Finally, from a cleared platform at the top of the Hill Complex, two large stones (approximately 5 meters in height) in close proximity to each other can be seen to form a slit directed precisely east which could have served as a solar marker for the equinoxes.

Doyle does, however, stress that further scholarly verification is required before a definitive conclusion can be made:

These and other observations are, however, preliminary and a better understanding of the calendrical systems of the early inhabitants of this region would substantially improve further investigations into any astronomical features that may have been built into the ruins at Great Zimbabwe.

Ethiopia

The Namoratunga II evidence from Kenya shows a close connection to the astronomical discoveries of some of the people in Ethiopia. The connection is so close that many scholars consider the Kenyan and Ethiopian evidence to be the same intellectual heritage. The Ethiopians concerned are the Borana people, a subgroup of the Oromo people.

Professor Asmarom Legesse, the distinguished Eritrean anthropologist, was amongst the first to recognise the calendrical system used by the Borana people. He wrote 'Borana have an unusually deep awareness of time and history ... they have the same degree of involvement with time as we find in the western world. They schedule life crisis ceremonies to a degree that would be inconceivable to the most time-conscious Western cultures.'

As with the Namoratunga II data, scholars believe that the Borana calendar was developed in 300 BC. The calendar is based upon the phases of the moon. The Borana year is made up of 12 months that are 29.5 days long; this makes a year of 354 days which is 11 days shorter than a solar year. The twelve lunar months have the following names: Cikawa, Sadasa, Abrasa, Maji, Gurrandala, Biottottessa, Camsa, Bufa, Wacabajji, Obora Gudda, Obora ikka and Birra. Their months contain no weeks but has the names of 27 days; days 28-30 repeat themselves in each lunar month.

Professor Legesse writes:

> A Borana time-reckoning expert (Ayyantu) can tell the day, the month, the year, and the gada period from memory. Should his memory fail him, he examines the relative position of the stars and the moon to determine the day and the month astronomically. The seven stars or constellations he uses are: *Lami* (Triangulum), *Busan* (Pleiades), *Bakkalcha* (Aldebaran), *Algajima* (Bellatrix), *Arb Gaddu* (central cluster of Orion), *Urji Wala* (Saiph) and *Basa* (Sirius).

Other information on early Ethiopian astronomy comes from two sets of source information. Some of the Ethiopian manuscripts contain astronomical texts that are related to the Book of Enoch. Other manuscripts contain tables and formulae to enable the calculation of Christian festivals such as Easter. Professor Otto Neugebauer made a special study of these documents. The manuscripts dated from the fourteenth to the nineteenth centuries. Since they were copies of older manuscripts Neugebauer could not give solid dates to the originals. There was one clear exception to this. Neugebauer explains: 'It is, however, a singularly fortunate accident that we have an Ethiopic table that can be dated to the years Diocletian 27 to 85 (A. D. 311 to 369).'

The manuscripts show that the Ethiopians freely drew upon astronomical ideas and concepts from the Coptic Egyptians, Greeks and Arabs. Some manuscripts show basic knowledge of the five planets (Mercury, Venus, Mars, Saturn and Jupiter). Some of these have diagrams of planetary periods. Others describe the 28 lunar mansions and include diagrams. However, some of these manuscripts contain misunderstandings of these concepts too. They did not use the mansions to tell the time at night as was done in Timbuktu. Other manuscripts show the 12 signs or towers of the Zodiac, some also with diagrams. The Ethiopians combined the 12 gates from the Book of Enoch with the Zodiacal signs from Arabic and Latin sources. Some manuscripts describe lunar phases and lunar illumination, again some with diagrams. Other manuscripts mention solar eclipses in 1241 AD, 1528 and 1727. A manuscript mentions a lunar eclipse in 1620. An Ethiopian (and also a Chinese) manuscript recorded the appearance of a nova in 1618.

Thus the Ethiopians calculated a 354 day lunar year, a 364 day Enoch year, and a 365 day solar year with the 366 day leap year. What the Ethiopians never did, however, was to synthesize the different material (Coptic, Greek and Arabic) into a single coherent body of astronomy. Professor Neugebauer is also scathing about the fact that Ethiopia never advanced astronomy beyond the arithmetic necessary to maintain the Christian and Jewish calendars.

The Ethiopians drew up 532 year tables which combined much of these calculations for their religious calendars. However, Professor Neugebauer conceded that: 'the practical arrangement of the tables which had to provide the user with the dates both of Passover and of Easter and of the associated feast days shows real skill and understanding of the arithmetic structure of the relevant numerical sequences.'

However Professor Neugebauer cited one example from an Amharic manuscript which must have been original to the Ethiopian scribe who wrote it since 'the value for the lunar month ... is not known to me [i.e. Neugebauer] from any published source.' The manuscript gave the mean value of a synodic month as 29:31,50,7,57,30d. This is a base 60 division of a mean lunar month into $29 + 31/60 + 50/60^2 + 7/60^3 + 57/60^4 + 30/60^5$ days. This is a brilliant calculation. Wikipedia gives the correct figure as 29 days, 12 hours, 44 minutes and 2.8 seconds.

In modern times, the legacy of Ethiopian astronomy has been recognised internationally. In May 2019, Space In Africa reported that Ethiopia had been given naming rights to some celestial bodies by the International Astronomical Union. The article reads:

> in celebration of the hard work and significant contributions of Ethiopians to the world of astronomy, the International Astronomical Union (IAU) is assigning to the country (through Ethiopian Space Science and Technology Institute (ESSTI) and Ethiopian Space Science Society (ESSS) the naming right to some celestial bodies which include a star (HD16175) and a planet (HD16175b).

CHAPTER 4: MEDICINE AND SURGERY

Ancient Egypt

The Ancient Greek poet, Homer, stated that: 'In medical knowledge, Egypt leaves the rest of the world behind.' According to the Ancient Egyptian historian Manetho, Pharaoh Djer (5581-5524 BC), of the First Dynasty, wrote a book on anatomy. The same historian reported that Pharaoh Djet (5507-5476 BC), also of the First Dynasty, wrote a famous medical text. Scholars today believe they have identified the Djet era text. They think it has survived as the *Edwin Smith Surgical Papyrus.*

The *Edwin Smith Papyrus* is now housed in the New York Academy of Medicine. It was one of ten surviving Ancient Egyptian medical texts. It describes 48 cases of bone surgery and of external pathology. It demonstrates a detailed knowledge of anatomy, gives remarkably accurate descriptions of traumatic surgical lesions, and describes their treatments where applicable.

Though written during the Eighteenth Egyptian Dynasty, it is a copy of a much older Egyptian text. The Eighteenth Dynasty copyist included glossaries for the readers because the original language nearly 3,000 years earlier was just too archaic.

What has survived is only one third of the original manuscript that stops at the 48th case. Consequently, it deals only with the skeletal and soft tissue parts of the head and neck, i.e. the upper portion of the body. It uses nearly 100 anatomical terms in the head and neck regions. Each case is written out as (i) an examination, (ii) a diagnosis, (iii) a treatment (iv) and finally, glossaries to explain the First Dynasty language to an Eighteenth Dynasty surgeon.

Professor Charles Finch, a medical doctor, who has made a special study of the contents of this papyrus, was somewhat baffled by the standards of medical knowledge achieved. He notes that: 'Cases 29-33 all represent additional case descriptions of vertebral dislocations and sub-luxations and their clinical consequences. At present, some of these conditions are almost impossible to detect or describe fully without X-ray studies. The question then arises is how did our ancient surgeon, living a[n]d practicing

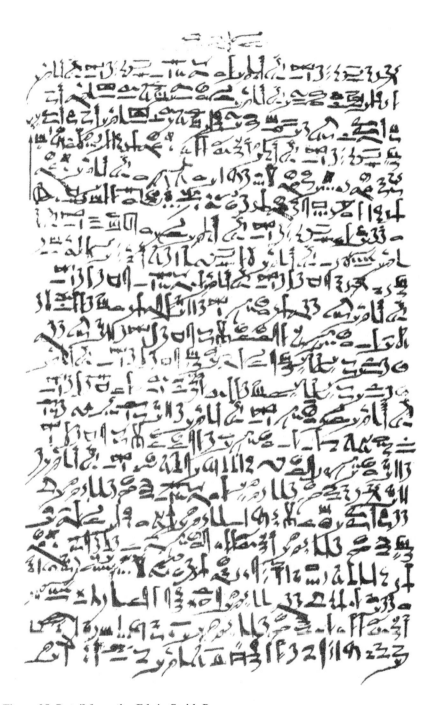

Figure 25. Detail from the *Edwin Smith Papyrus.*

[thousands of] years ago, manage to diagnose and describe these problems without benefit of X-rays?' To answer Professor Finch, we just don't know.

Professor Théophile Obenga was also impressed with this document. Case 31 deals with a fracture causing a dislocation of the cervical vertebrae. This led to quadriplegia in the patient. This case demonstrates that the Egyptians understood the connections between injuries to the central nervous system and peripheral damage elsewhere. This implies they recognised the unity of the nervous system and the interconnection of central and peripheral nerves.

Professor Finch informs us that the Ancient Egyptians had a total of perhaps 200 terms for the different parts of the human body that appear in their papyri. There are Ancient Egyptian terms for bones of the head--the cranium, cranial vault, cranial sutures, suture membrane, superciliary arch, orbit, mandibular notch, the internal auditory canal and the external auditory canal. There are terms for the soft tissue parts including the meninges, cerebrum, convolutions of the brain, nasal fossa, nasal cartilage, pharynx, spinal cord, larynx, and oesophagus. For the skeleton, there are terms for the manubrium, sternum, patella, clavicles, scapula, humerus and thoracic vertebra. For the internal organs, there are terms for the liver, intestine, lung, pericardium, stomach, spleen, pancreas, kidney and bladder. Finally there are terms for cerebral spinal fluid, the blood vessel network, the spinal-cord, et cetera.

It should also be borne in mind that with thousands of years of practising mummification, the Ancient Egyptians amassed an array of knives, scalpels and surgical techniques. They used red hot implements to seal off bleeding. They closed wounds with adhesive tape or sutures. Mummification itself took a team of skilled medical personnel perhaps 70 days to complete. Among the many actions needed to complete a mummification, involved evisceration, removing the brain, desiccation, washing the body inside and out using natron, anointing the purified body with aromatic oils and herbs, and wrapping the body in endless bandages. Among the chemical substances involved in the process were palm wine, various spices, perfumes, myrrh, aniseed, onions and natron.

Professor Théophile Obenga was very impressed with the *Ebers Papyrus* and describes it as humanity's first medical encyclopaedia. It has chapters on intestinal disease, ophthalmology, dermatology, gynaecology, obstetrics, pregnancy diagnosis, contraception, dentistry, surgical treatment of abscesses, tumours, fractures and burns. The Papyrus has a section on the movement of the heart and pulse cited from and older text called *The Book*

Figure 26. Detail of a wall carving showing a person setting a dislocated shoulder.

of the Heart and Vessels. This document describes how the heart pumps blood around the body. What it did not say was that the blood returns to the heart. It was this discovery that made William Harvey, the seventeenth century English scholar, famous. The Papyrus also describes in arcane and picturesque language certain heart ailments such as angina pectoris and Stokes-Adams attacks. Finally, the *Ebers Papyrus* has a section on diagnostic percussion.

Some earlier writers were of the opinion that the Egyptians knew nothing about the function of the brain. Professor Finch points out that Egyptian art shows the raised serpent coming out of the vertex of the cranium on the Pharaonic headdress. He believes that the position of the serpent symbolically divides the cranium into two equal halves or hemispheres. Moreover, the Ancient Egyptian word for the cranial vertex is *wpt* which means to open, to discern, or to judge. The Ancient Egyptian word for cerebrum is *âmm* and means to know and to understand. This shows that the Egyptians knew that the brain was connected to knowing, understanding, judging, and discernment. Professor Obenga points out that Case 22 of the *Edwin Smith Papyrus* shows that brain damage can impair a patient's ability to speak.

In the Old Kingdom Period (i.e. Dynasty One to Six), the doctors were specialists--they focussed on just the eyes, head, teeth, or intestines, etcetera. There was even a separate guild of bone setters who treated fractures and dislocations and pioneered the very same techniques that Hippocrates, the Ancient Greek scholar, would popularise thousands of years later. The Egyptian medical doctors were employed by the state. One Old Kingdom position was 'Chief of Dentists and Physicians.' Another position was 'Director of the Women Doctors.'

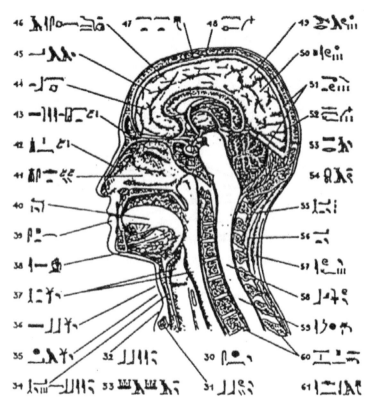

Figure 27. The Ancient Egyptians had anatomical terms for parts of the brain and other anatomical features of the head, many of which have been identified here.

Incidentally, nearly 120 physicians appear in the Egyptian annals. Typically, they were trained in an institution called the 'per ankh.' At once, this served as a school, library, clinic, temple and seminary. Much of the teaching and training was taught orally as was done elsewhere in Africa.

Described in both the *Edwin Smith* and the *Ebers Papyri,* the Ancient Egyptian doctors pioneered the use of the diagnostic method. Thus, the patient describes the complaint to the doctor. The doctor then assessed the patient checking over the face, the eyes, nasal secretions, perspiration, and testing for stiffness of limbs or the abdomen. The doctor would ask for a urine and a faeces sample. They took the patients pulse. We know that the Egyptians invented the hour but they must also have invented smaller units of time. Did they invent the minute and the second also? Finally, the doctor percussed the abdomen or chest of the patient.

Figure 28. Statuette of Imhotep, the great Third Dynasty era Prime Minister, Architect and Medical Doctor. He has handsome African features typical of the Ancient Egyptians during this period of history.

The Ancient Egyptians used a *Materia Medica* of 1,000 animal, plant and mineral products. This is a large pharmacopeia since they could also combine these animal, plant and mineral products. They used moulds from bread, i.e. from the penicillium family, internally and externally to treat infections. Thus, they created the first antibiotic. They used poppy extract, i.e. opium, to treat colicky babies and as a sedative and pain killer. They used ox livers, rich in vitamin A, to treat night blindness. They used onions, rich in vitamin C, to treat scurvy. They used mandrake or related plants for sedation and to treat eye disorders. They used honey combined with grease as a wound salve. This has been shown to speed up the healing of wounds and reduce infections. Finally, they dispensed prescriptions as pills, enemas, suppositories and elixirs.

Imhotep, a Third Dynasty Prime Minister, was the first great individual in recorded history. Before him, history was strictly about Gods and Kings. Imhotep was an intellectual of wide interests including medicine. In western culture, it has become customary to give credit to the Greek scholar Hippocrates as the pioneering medical doctor. Medical practitioners today have the option of swearing on the Hippocratic Oath to promise that they will do no harm to their patients. However, the Oath is dedicated to the gods Apollo and Aesculapius. Aesculapius is none other than Imhotep!

Even more embarrassing, Professor Cheikh Anta Diop reports the following information:

> Theophrastus, Dioscorides, and Galen perpetually cite the prescriptions that they received from the Egyptian physicians, or more specifically, as Galen says, that they had learned by consulting the works conserved in the library of the Temple of Imhotep at Memphis, which was still accessible in the second century A.D., and where, seven centuries before, Hippocrates, the "father of medicine" was taught.

The Ancient Egyptians also invented a contraceptive solution. It was a concoction whose active ingredient was a spermicide that did actually kill sperm.

They also pioneered a pregnancy test which involved sprinkling urine of a possibly pregnant woman on barley to test how the barley grew. Modern scholars say this test was 40% successful. This is a low figure, but we must remember that modern pregnancy tests are far from reliable!

Kush and Nubia

Professor Charles Finch wrote a classic essay on early African medicine and surgery entitled *The African Background to the Medical Science.* In this splendid 1983 essay, he gave startling examples of early East African medicine and surgery. In 1980, a scholar published a paper called *Tetracycline-Labeled Bone from Ancient Sudanese Nubia.* The paper appeared in *Science* magazine. The main finding was the discovery that early Mediaeval Nubian skeletons from 350 to 550 AD were found to have had tetracycline in their bones. However, the author of the paper did not know why this was the case. Professor Finch, by contrast, drew the conclusion from the same evidence that the tetracycline was used in such a quantity that suggested that its use was deliberate and pharmaceutical. Tetracycline is an antibiotic which derives from a mould belonging to the streptomyces family.

Later research, however, has found that the use of tetracycline in this region dated back to an even earlier period. Its use could be traced back to Kushite times.

West Africa

In 1420 a Songhai doctor, Aben Ali, successfully treated the French crown prince, later King Charles VII when all else failed. Secondly, in 1492 the great Songhai emperor Sunni Ali Ber was mummified. These two examples tell us something of the high standards of medical and surgical knowledge in West Africa in the fifteenth century.

Mahmud Kati, a Songhai historian, mentions the use of locally manufactured soap. A surviving sixteenth century Timbuktu manuscript has a formula for making toothpaste and adds that regular brushing of your teeth removes bad breath. Other surviving manuscripts deal with chemistry, traditional medicines and pharmacopoeia.

Moreover, Professor Diop shows how the West Africans organised medical practice at that time: 'Empirical medicine was quite developed in Africa ... a family practised a single branch of medicine on an hereditary basis. One was specialised in the eyes, the stomach, and so on."

Professor Charles Finch, associate professor of medicine at Morehouse, demonstrated that West African countries traditionally used a large range of plants, minerals and animal material for medical purposes. Some groups, such as the Mano of Liberia, practiced quarantining to contain diseases. West Africans used local anaesthetics and had treatments for asthma, bronchitis, diabetes, malaria and muscular-skeletal pain. They used plants that had anti-sickle cell properties and other plants that had insect repellent properties.

Azadirachta indica, or the Neem tree, grows widely across Africa. Healers traditionally used its bark and leaves to treat malaria and to reduce muscular-skeletal pain. Tinctures derived from the Neem tree have greater anti-inflammatory properties than aspirin. *Bridelia ferruginea* is an effective treatment for diabetes. One study produced examples where some patients' blood sugar levels returned to normal after taking the treatment for twelve weeks. *Zanthoxulum zanthoxlides,* or the chewing stick, effectively cleans teeth and combats tooth decay. It also has anti sickle-cell properties. *Ocimum gratissimum* treats diarrhoea. It also has insect repellent properties. For this reason, many people grew this plant near their homes. *Pergularia daema* has multiple uses. It functioned as a post-circumcision anaesthetic. It was also a topical treatment for abscesses and wounds. *Euphorbita hirta* treats asthma and bronchitis.

Benaebi Benatari gives the specific examples of the Yoruba of Ijebu and the Ijo. They practiced massage, bone surgery and herbalism to a highly developed degree. They washed then bandaged dead bodies in layers and layers of bandages and cloth with the two hands of the dead individual brought together.

Another specific example was in the Kingdom of Senegal. A European testified at a British Government Select Committee in 1790 that Senegalese physicians had a *materia medica* of 2,000 or nearly 3,000 plants. This, incidentally, is a pharmacopeia two and a half times as extensive as that of the Ancient Egyptians.

It may surprise most readers but it remains a fact that the majority of enslaved Africans were inoculated against smallpox BEFORE they were deported from Africa. The Mano of Liberia were among a number of West African peoples that invented a smallpox vaccine before the Europeans. Susan McIntosh and Roderick McIntosh, both experts on Ancient Mali, state that West African blacksmiths, such as the Bambara, also developed a smallpox vaccine before the Europeans. One enslaved African in Boston, Onesimus, taught the treatment to his enslaver in the 1720s.

The University of Djenné taught surgery in mediaeval times. One area of specialism was eye cataract surgery.

Kenya, Tanzania and Uganda

Professor Finch points out that surgery in East Africa was traditionally at a high level. Traditional surgeons among the Massai of Kenya and Tanzania performed limb amputations and devised prostheses for severed limbs.

Some interesting information has survived about the 19th-century Kingdom of Banyoro in what is today known as Uganda. Medical practitioners in this kingdom routinely carried out autopsies on patients dying of unknown causes. A British medical doctor in 1879 witnessed an event that was quite extraordinary--a Caesarean section. In Europe Caesarean sections performed at the time had a 100% death rate for the mother. Dr R. W. Felkin witnessed a surgeon in Banyoro accompanied by two assistants carrying out a Caesarean section. The surgeon used anaesthetics, antiseptics, effective surgical techniques, and the sparing use of cautery iron to reduce bleeding. When Felkin left the kingdom to return home ten days later, both mother and baby were doing well. A few years

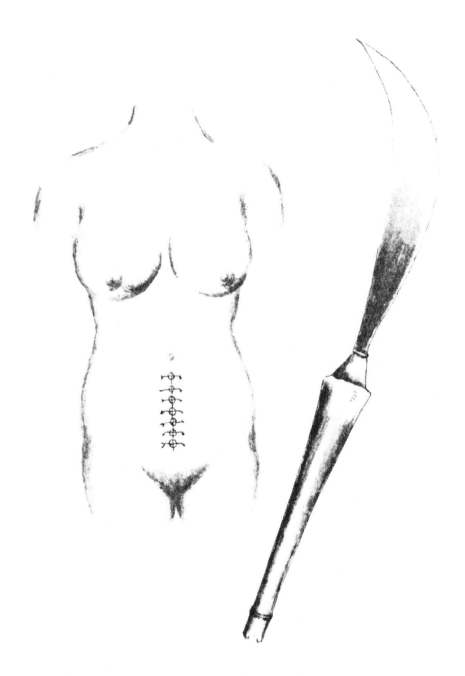

Figure 29. Knife and post caesarean wound derived from Dr R. W. Felkin's description, drawn by Sylvia Bakos.

later, Felkin wrote up what he witnessed in Uganda and his article appeared in an 1884 edition of the *Edinburgh Medical Journal.*

Other than the Finch essay, two splendid works have shed greater light on African medicine and surgery. Professor Richard Pankhurst wrote the splendid *An Introduction to the Medical History of Ethiopia.* Published in 1990, the book documented the medical and surgical practices of early Ethiopia and Somalia. Dr A. T. Bryant compiled the exquisite *Zulu Medicine and Medicine-Men* over many years in the late nineteenth and early twentieth centuries. Finally published in 1966 and 1983, the book drew many radical conclusions. For example, according to Dr Bryant: 'It is by no means an exaggeration to affirm that comparatively the average Zulu can boast of a larger share of pure scientific knowledge than the average European.'

Somalia

According to Professor Richard Pankhurst, Somali traditional medicine and surgery shared some features with the Ethiopian. They used counterirritation almost as a panacea. They used fumigation in the treating of ill patients by covering them with hot sand and placing aromatics under their bed. They used purgatives and also sulphur to treat syphilis. Most importantly, they were excellent bone setters. They set fractures by supporting them with twigs and reeds woven together. They were even able to insert bones from sheep into humans.

Zulu

According to Dr A. T. Bryant, most traditional medical practitioners among the Zulu followed their fathers into the profession. Initially, the sons worked as their father's assistants. They worked as his messengers, herb gatherers, and general helpers. They accompanied their fathers on his excursions as a medicine-bearer, picking up by instruction and observation, medical knowledge and skills. After many years as an assistant, the young man might strike out by himself and establish his own practice. He typically shared remedies with neighbouring doctors and grew in knowledge and expertise through the practice of consulting. After twenty years or more, he learned all there was to learn about the Zulu pharmacopeia and local pathology.

The medical practitioners were called *i-nyanga* in Zulu and *i-nyangi* in Xhosa. Their knowledge and practice covered medicine but also overlapped with the arts associated with priests and diviners. In Zulu society, however, there was a distinction between the *i-nyanga yokwelapha* (the doctor for curing) and the *i-nyanga yokubhula* (the doctor for divining).

Dr Bryant was scornful about the poor state of Zulu knowledge of human anatomy and physiology. Knowledge of the nervous system seemed close to nil. However the Zulu doctors were conversant with symptoms and diseases. According to Dr Bryant, the key rule seems to have been that there were as many diseases as there were symptoms. This is not an entirely acceptable methodology, since the same condition could cause multiple symptoms! Amongst the drug therapies used were drastic astringents and, as elsewhere, drastic purgatives.

Dr Bryant documented the names of 225 plants used in Zulu medicine. Andrew Smith, another authority wrote on 150 plants used by the Xhosa and Fingo. Smith also mentions another 240 plants in Zulu medical use. In total there were around 700 plants used in Zulu medicine. In addition, the pharmacopeia covered a wide range from the mineral, vegetable and animal kingdoms, terrestrial and marine.

Dr Bryant says:

> In spite of such blind empiricism it cannot be denied that the native doctor does sometimes work a cure, sometimes quite a startling cure, where the efforts of European physicians have proved utterly unavailing. Remedies he has ... without number, and some of them truly helpful, suited to every ill--physical, mental, moral and social--that man is heir to. Frequently it is to these we may attribute his success.

However, some of the other successes were based on the placebo effect. In the opinion of Dr Bryant, 'many ... cures, and, it may be added, of many ... ailments, is not the action of matter on matter, of drug on flesh, but in those occult regions where mind works on mind and mind on flesh.'

According to Dr Bryant, the traditional Zulu methods of preparing medicines 'are much like our own.' Medicines were given as cold infusions that combined cold water with the chopped or powdered medicine. Some were given as hot infusions prepared like tea. Others were decoctions that were simmered. Some were given as powders. Some medicines were applied topically as liquids, ointments, lotions, and powders. As elsewhere, the Zulus had vapour and sweating baths. Finally, the Zulus practiced blood-letting, an idea widely practised in many countries, even in Europe.

The Zulu doctors had treatments for a wide range of ailments. Dr Bryant details the plant materials used in the treatment of broken limbs and sprains, catarrh, chest pains, chronic coughing, dropsy, dry cough, earache, eczema, expectoration of blood, extraction of thorns, febrile complaints, gangrenous rectitis, gonorrhoea, headache, heartburn, heart complaints, impotence, indigestion, infantile thrush, intercostal neuralgia, intestinal parasites, kidney disease, measles, nausea, ophthalmia, paralysis, piles, pleurisy, rheumatism, scrofula, skin sores, smallpox, snake bites, spinal disease, stomach and intestinal complaints, syphilis, tapeworm, toothache, urinary complaints, and wounds.

They also had treatments for 'barrenness', 'insanity' and 'hysteria.' Less controversially, they also had prescriptions that produced a hair dye. They also had a vermin killer.

In summary, Bryant found that some of the traditional Zulu medicines and medical procedures were worthless and even dangerous. On the other hand, he found that Zulu doctors were familiar 'with certain curative herbs and plants long before the Western medical world learned about these.'

Ethiopia

Ethiopia possesses a small but important number of medical manuscripts. Written in Ge'ez and Amharic, these texts date from the second half of the eighteenth century. Others were from the nineteenth and early twentieth centuries. Broad in nature, the texts cover illnesses, diseases and their treatments. They also cover and combine issues of a magical nature such as averting the evil eye, overcoming evil spirits, defeating your enemies, etcetera.

The scientific content of these texts describe treatments for epilepsy, fever, syphilis, rabies, skin diseases, kidney problems, haemorrhoids, constipation, diarrhoea, dysuria, itching, coughing, sterility and even snoring. The texts describe thousands of prescriptions that involved an extensive pharmacopeia derived from the vegetable, animal and mineral kingdoms.

Visitors to Ethiopia from the seventeenth to the nineteenth centuries reported how the Ethiopians controlled the spread of epidemics like smallpox, cholera, typhus and influenza. They retired to the mountainous areas at the first evidence of an outbreak of disease. They prevented the movement of people to and from affected areas. They prevented the movement of cattle in the case of cattle diseases. They even burned the sick alive in their houses in extreme cases.

Visitors also describe how the Ethiopians used counterirritation by burning as a medical technique. One visitor described it as 'very efficacious.' They treated inflammation of the lungs by making small burns on the chest. They also treated rheumatism using similar techniques.

Another technique frequently used was cautery. They used it to disinfect skin. It was used to prevent bleeding and also used in the treatment of scorpion bites, snake bites and bites from other creatures.

The Ethiopians successfully practised the inoculation of populations against smallpox. They attempted similar inoculation techniques for the treatment of rabies and syphilis. They combined the attempted inoculation techniques with a range of other treatments.

In the case of rabies, Ethiopian manuscripts from the eighteenth century specifically mention that a bite from a rabid dog was often fatal. It was thus a serious condition requiring urgent attention. Nineteenth century manuscripts show that the Ethiopians were aware that the incubation period for rabies was 40 days. After carefully cleaning and disinfecting the wound, they treated rabies by using a range of purgatives. Purgatives were prescriptions designed to deliberately induce vomiting or diarrhoea in the patient.

In the case of syphilis, the Ethiopians traditionally prescribed a range of purgatives but also taenicides. Taenicides were prescriptions that killed tapeworms in the stomach which was also supposed to help in combating syphilis. *Ximenia americana* was rated highly by the Ethiopians as a topical treatment for syphilitic sores. Sometimes the prescriptions were combined with bathing in thermal springs. With temperatures of between 49 and 60 degrees Celsius, naturally occurring thermal springs were also thought to be efficacious in the treatment of rheumatism, arthritis, skin diseases, wounds and leprosy.

Ethiopians living near the Sudanese border consumed mercury rich earth with water or applied it topically to treat syphilis. The efficacy of mercury in the treatment of syphilis has been noted around the world. In Gondar vapour baths were established. These were specially constructed stone buildings that were kept very hot. The syphilitic patient stayed in this hot environment and was prescribed sarsaparilla or mercury--treatments also in use in Europe nearly a hundred years earlier.

Surgery was practised extensively and covered simple and complex operations. A nineteenth century visitor wrote that they 'excelled in surgery' and displayed 'truly amazing' skill and courage. They extracted tonsils. They even opened the stomach, took out intestines, cleaned them and replaced them in the stomach. They routinely carried out amputations that involved cutting the skin and the tendons, followed by the ligaments.

The wound was covered by powders, cinders or leaves. Alternatively, they were cauterised using hot irons. Surgeons in Tegré performed Caesarean sections for difficult childbirths.

Bone setting was practised and with a high degree of success. Splints were made of bone or wood. In Harar they made plates of iron, lead or copper. Fractured skulls were often treated by replacing damaged parts of a skull by bones from goats or sheep.

CHAPTER 5: ARCHITECTURE

Ancient Egypt

Architecture is a combination of art and technology and often encompasses the uses of many other sciences in their constructions. A typical building is analysed by its plan, its walling which includes the building materials, the openings (i.e. the doorways and windows), the supports, the roofing, and the ornamentation.

Pharaoh Djoser, the second king of the Third Egyptian Dynasty, ruled between 5018 and 4989 BC. He built the earliest monument in the world still celebrated today. Every year, thousands of tourists visit his Funerary Complex in the city of Saqqara. Imhotep, his celebrated Prime Minister, designed the Complex.

An outer wall, now mostly in ruins, surrounded the whole structure. It was built on a rectangular plan, one mile long, and with one entrance. Through the entrance are a series of columns, the first stone-built columns known to historians. Connected to walls, they are ornamental having been modelled on plant stems grouped together. The North House also has ornamental columns built into the walls that have papyrus-like capitals. Also inside the complex is the Ceremonial Court. Like everything else these buildings are solid and are thus symbolic. The Court is made of limestone blocks that have been quarried and then shaped. In the centre of the complex is the Step Pyramid, the first of 90 Egyptian pyramids. Made of limestone blocks, it is 197 feet high. Unlike the later pyramids, this structure is built on a rectangular plan measuring 345 by 414 feet - equivalent to a base of 14,000 square yards. It has 6 steps and may represent a stairway. The building slopes at an angle of 72° 30'. Under the Pyramid were a series of rock-hewn chambers and corridors. They are ornamented with panels of colourful tiles. In these hidden quarters, Djoser and eleven others are said to have been buried. On the importance of the Djoser Complex, Professor Finch noted that: '[It] was humanity's first great architectural triumph. It established architectural forms, styles, and canons still in use today. The practical building technique and masonry evident in the entrance temple were never surpassed, though ... they were realized on a grander scale.'

Figure 30. Detail from the North House of the Saqqara Complex. This monument contains the first attempt to build columns in human history.

Figure 31. Plan of a part of Kahun, showing houses of similar layouts and streets laid out on a horizontal vertical grid.

The monuments 'on a grander scale' include the structures built by the Fourth Dynasty Pharaohs - the Step Pyramid of Meidum, the Bent and Red Pyramids of Dashur, and the three Great Pyramids of Giza - monuments built between 4872 and 4615 BC. Of these, the most impressive is the first Great Pyramid of Giza. It was 481 feet tall, the equivalent of a 40 storey building. It was made of 2.3 million blocks of limestone and granite, some weighing 100 tons. The accuracy of the construction work remains astonishing. Dr Alfred Russell Wallace, a famous British scientist, commented on this more than a hundred years ago in an address before the British Association for the Advancement of Science:

1. That the pyramid is truly square, the sides being equal, and the angles right angles; 2. That the four sockets on which the first four stones of the corners

rested are truly on the same level; 3. That the directions of the sides are accurate to the four cardinal points [of north, south, east and west]; 4. That the vertical height of the pyramid bears the same proportion to its circumference at the base as the radius of a circle does to its circumference [i.e. the Egyptians understood π].

Pharaoh Senwosret II (3331-3299 BC) of the Middle Kingdom constructed Kahun, a town of officials, priests and workers. It had over a hundred houses where even the smallest homes for people of the lowest rank had 4 to 6 rooms and an area of 1,022 square feet or larger.

Excavations revealed that this city was the world's first known example of town planning. Kahun was rectangular and walled. Inside, the city was divided into two parts. One part housed the wealthier inhabitants - the scribes, officials and foremen. The other part housed the ordinary people. The streets of the western section in particular, were straight, laid out on a grid, and crossed each other at right angles. A stone gutter, over half a metre wide, ran down the centre of every street. Positioned to benefit from the cool north winds, five single storey mansions were found along the northern edge of the city. Their doorways were arched. Each boasted 70 rooms, divided into four sections or quarters. There was a master's quarter, quarters for women and servants, quarters for offices and finally, quarters for granaries, each facing a central courtyard. The master's quarters had an open court with a stone water tank for bathing. Surrounding this was a colonnade. Of the maze of rooms, some were barrel vaulted in brick but others were wooden and thatched. The ceilings were supported by wooden and stone columns some with palmiform capitals. Limewash coated the walls, but some rooms contained frescoes.

Amenemhet III (3242-3195 BC) of the same dynasty built at Hawara the Labyrinth with its massive layout, multiple courtyards, chambers and halls. The very largest building in antiquity, it boasted 3,000 rooms. One thousand five hundred were above ground and the other one thousand five hundred were underground. Herodotus, the Ancient Greek historian, saw it in ruins three thousand years later. He was still somewhat impressed:

> I visited this place, and found it to surpass description; for if all the walls and other great works of the Greeks could be put together in one, they would not equal, either for labour or expense, this Labyrinth; and yet the [Greek] temple of Ephesus is a building worthy of note, and so is the temple of Samos. The pyramids likewise surpass description, and are equal to a number of the greatest works of the Greeks; but the Labyrinth surpasses the pyramids.

Further south, lay the complex of temples in the city of Waset. The

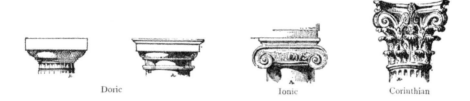

Doric Ionic Corinthian

Figure 32. It is not difficult to trace the development of architecture from the Saqqara Complex, through the Karnak Complex to the evolution of Greek architecture. Greek capitals are typically classified as Doric, Ionic or Corinthian.

Karnak and Luxor temples, now in partial ruin, were built over many years with contributions from different pharaohs of the Twelfth, Eighteenth, Nineteenth and Twenty-Fifth Dynasties (3405-664 BC). The Karnak Complex was a place of culture and business. It should be thought of as an abbey since people lived and worked there and the complex was self-contained. The treasures of the ancient world passed through its corridors; gold and precious woods from Kush, tribute from Syria, and vases from Crete. A procession of sphinxes led to the outer pylon, itself 370 feet across, 143 feet high, and 49 feet thick at the base, but becoming narrower at the top. Behind the pylon was the Temple of Amen, which originally had huge doors to close it off. A place of unbelievable luxury, the Hypostyle Hall, just one of its many temples, was 171 feet long and 338 feet wide, covering an area of 56,000 square feet. It was the largest enclosed space in Egyptian architecture, even larger than Durham Cathedral by 5,000 square feet. It contained 134 sandstone columns, covered with bas-reliefs and hieroglyphics. An architect described the Hall as follows:

> No language [says Fergusson] can convey an idea of its beauty, and no artist has yet been able to reproduce its form so as to convey to those who have not seen it any ideas of its grandeur. The mass of its central piers, illuminated by a flood of light from the clerestory, and the smaller pillars of the wings gradually fading into obscurity, are so arranged and lighted as to convey an idea of infinite space; at the same time the beauty and massiveness of the forms, and the brilliancy of their coloured decorations, all combine to stamp this as *the greatest of man's architectural works.*

There were huge obelisks that stood before the façades of the Karnak and Luxor temples. They were made of a single piece of stone that was hewn from a quarry and then transported to the required position. Pharaoh

Hatshepsut erected one such obelisk. It was 90.2 feet tall and weighed an astonishing 302 tons. There is a huge and unfinished obelisk that is 41.78 metres long that was left at Aswan, presumably because it did not meet exacting standards of accuracy. The importance of these monuments are such that one authority has argued that there is a typological and symbolic link between the obelisks of ancient times and the skyscrapers of today. As Dr Nnamdi Elleh, an expert in African architecture, put it: 'Several texts exist of Pharaohs boasting that they erected obelisks which reached, pierced, or mingled with the sky.'

Pharaoh Hatshepsut (1650-1600 BC) of the Eighteenth Dynasty was also the builder of one of Egypt's most popular monuments. Senenmut, the Overseer of Works, constructed her temple in the region now known as Deir-el-Bahri.

Rather than build upwards from a base, the Mortuary Temple was built downwards, being cut out of a mountain. The whole building was hewn from the rocks by hammer and chisel. The result is a pillared terrace structure that rises in three stages with 2 central ramps, also carved and sculpted. The ramps are long and slope with a gentle gradient. Their position divides the temple into two symmetrical halves. Entrance halls of limestone columns lead to the interior chapels dedicated to the deities Anubis, Hathor, Osiris and Ra. Through the colonnade, the interior has wall reliefs that depict Hatshepsut's maritime voyages to Punt (i.e. possibly Somalia or Ethiopia) showing also the round houses of that country. In its time, great sculptures embellished the building. There were over 100 limestone sphinxes, 22 granite sphinxes, 40 limestone statues of Hatshepsut, and 28 granite statues of Hatshepsut.

Rameses II of the Nineteenth Dynasty also built a temple carved out of a hill. The Temple of Abu Simbel, in Nubia, is of an incredible scale. The façade is 108 feet wide and contains four colossal statues of the pharaoh, each 66 feet high. What is remarkable here is the organisational feat involved. The carved images of Rameses are so large that each builder/sculptor would be so close to their work that none of them would be able to see the bigger picture as they worked. For this reason, accuracy was critical and not just for artistic reasons. The building was oriented to the east to catch the first rays of sunlight that illuminated its icons at the end of a 208 feet corridor. Inside the entrance to the temple are statues of the deity Osiris. This led to a smaller hall that led to an inner chamber.

Kush

Kerma, the capital city of the Early Empire of Kush, was a particularly distinguished centre of architecture. The Empire of Kush was located in the same place as the modern Sudan and the southern portion of modern Egypt. Scholars divide the history of Kerma into the Ancient Period, the Middle Period and the Classic Period. These periods as a whole take us from the same time period as Dynasty VI Egypt to Dynasty XVIII Egypt. I controversially estimate the time period involved as *c.*4200 BC to 1601 BC.

Kerma, at the peak of its power was the largest city in Africa outside Egyptian territory, covering 65 acres. Surrounding the central parts of the city was a wall of massive size with a ditch in front of it. The walls were 30 feet high and made of mud bricks. They had rectangular towers that projected and also had four fortified gates.

Inside the city lay the gardens, the palace of the king, the houses of the nobility and the *deffufa,* a large white temple. It was 150 feet long, 75 feet wide, and a towering 60 feet tall. Its walls were 12 feet thick and were straight and even. There was also a second religious complex separated by a 16 foot wall. This complex consisted of bronze workshops, storerooms, housing for the priests, and also chapels.

Archaeologists working in the city have detected a large audience hall that probably dates from the Middle Period. This building was circular and may have been thatched. Also found were thousands of mud blanks that would have been used for making seals. This gives evidence that business transactions took place. There was also a great palace. It had an audience hall that included a throne on a raised platform. The king sat here and received delegations. Several large columns supported the roof and the building is believed to have been 25 feet high.

Kush flourished a second time between *c.*860 BC and 350 AD leaving behind a wealth of architectural evidence. There are at least 223 Kushite pyramids in the cities of Al Kurru, Nuri, Gebel Barkal and Meroë. They are generally 20 to 30 metres high and steep sided, sloping at around 70°. They were made of smaller blocks than their Egyptian counterparts. The pyramids were used for royal burials and were entered by underground stairways on the eastern side. Meroë became the capital of the Kushite Empire from around 590 BC until about 350 AD, a period well attested by monuments. There are, for example, 84 pyramids in this city alone, many built with their own miniature temple. Moreover, there are ruins of a bath house sharing affinities with those of the Romans.

Figure 33. Temple of Amen at Naqa. 1-20 AD. (Photo: Louis Buckley of Black Nine Films.)

In Musawarat there is a very large and curious complex generally called the Great Enclosure. Dated at 220 BC, it has a series of walled enclosures and edifices that surround a central temple, itself, built on a raised platform. Encircling the temple is a colonnade and outside of this is a series of ramps and corridors connecting the different parts of the building. Decorating the structure are elephant motifs.

The city of Naqa contains three important temples, the Temple of Amen, the Lion Temple, and the Kiosk. They date to between 1 AD and 20 AD. Kushite Pharaoh Natakamani and Queen Amanitore built the Temple of Amen and the Lion Temple. The Temple of Amen has a columned hall leading to an inner sanctuary as in Egyptian temples. In addition, there were 12 sculpted rams that lined the avenue to the entrance. The Lion Temple was dedicated to Apedemak, a local deity. It has a typical Egyptian-like pylon with the King and Queen depicted as conquerors bashing the heads of their enemies. The depiction of the Queen doing the same thing may represent a powerful role for the Queen or Queen Mother in the society or may even represent matriarchy. Behind the pylon is a one-room structure, a design unique to Kush. Finally, the Kiosk is a strange building that seems to have incorporated many cultural influences. There are arches, possibly reflecting Roman influence, and the capitals of the columns show traces of Greek influence. Some writers describe them as 'pseudo-Corinthian'. It is important to note, however, that there is no evidence that the Romans (or Greeks) built this temple. Many writers have hinted at this possibility, but in the absence of solid evidence, we must conclude that this is a Kushite monument built by Kushites.

Christian Nubia

The same Kushite region flourished a third time between the fourth century AD and the fourteenth or fifteenth centuries AD. For most of this period, the region consisted of two great Christian states--the Empire of Makuria to the north, and the Kingdom of Alwa to the south. Some scholars, such as the great Howard University social scientist, Chancellor Williams, regard this as the best period in the whole of Black history.

Archaeologists have found in Makuria and Alwa evidence of forts, castles, churches, monasteries, cathedrals, palaces, housing complexes with running water and water heating systems, toilets, and glass windows.

There were a number of fortified sites at Faras, Ikhmindi, Kalabsha, Sabaqura and Sheikh Daud. They had many features in common, both in

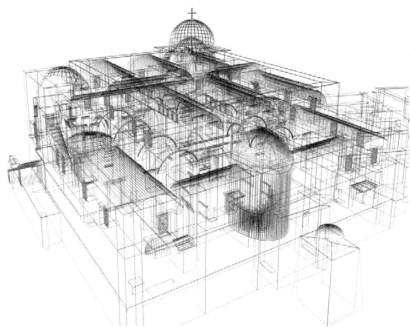

Figure 34. Polish archaeological restoration of the upper domed portion of Faras Cathedral, 707 AD. It is not difficult to see why some consider this 'the superior of many buildings of medieval Africa and the Near East.'

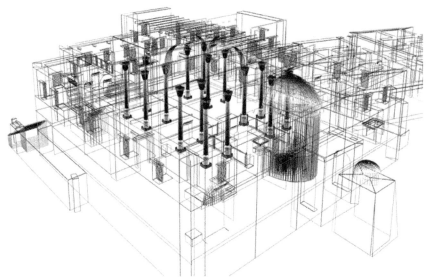

Figure 35. Polish archaeological restoration of the lower columned portion of Faras Cathedral.

their plan, and style of construction. Within the defences at Ikhmindi and Sheikh Daud, the layout of the buildings were remarkably regular and well planned. They had two roomed apartments that back onto the inner face of the defensive wall and were separated by a narrow street. The church occupied the central position. Other notable walled fortifications were at Bakhit, Diffar, Estabel, Jebel Deiga, Old Dongola, Selib and Sinada.

Faras was a much excavated city. It was found to have had defence walls that enclosed an area of 4.6 hectares. These walls were the largest building projects achieved in Medieval Nubia. The curtain wall was nearly 4m thick and 11.6m high. At the angles were substantial square external towers projecting 10m, while spaced at regular intervals along the curtain were slightly smaller towers. Two main gates survive in the centre of the south and west walls. Within these walls, there was a church of clay bricks constructed in the middle of the sixth century AD. Eventually, a cathedral was built on its site in 707 AD. The cathedral was a large five-aisle building covering 564 square metres and had Coptic and Greek inscriptions. In the tenth century AD the cathedral seems to have been damaged by fire. Two modern scholars, however, P. L. Shinnie and M. Shinnie, consider this building 'the superior of many buildings of medieval Africa and the Near East.' Also within the defensive circuit were three churches, two palatial structures, a monastery and an industrial complex that produced pottery. The two palaces date back to the seventh century AD and were linked by a narrow alleyway. They were certainly at least two storeys in height. Although built of mud brick, they had carved stone portals and the ground floor rooms were decorated with murals.

Qasr Ibrim was another important city. At one time, the hilltop contained churches, large areas of open piazza, a cemetery, and residences of important officials. An early visitor to the city wrote of its defensive wall and a 'large and beautiful church, finely planned and named after Our Lady the pure Virgin Mary. Above it is a high dome upon which rises a large cross.' This monument was probably built in the later half of the seventh century AD. It was a five-aisled basilica with a wide nave and apse. In size it measured 596 square metres. Beneath this building were crypts with barrel-vaults, 2m high, entered down two flights of stairs from the north and south outer aisles. The nave and aisles were paved with well-fitted stone slabs.

Arminna West and Debeira West were Nubian villages. Jakobielski, a Polish specialist in Christian archaeology, wrote that: 'Settlements investigated, such as Debeya [sic] West or Arminna, present a picture of a

Figure 36. Restored mediaeval Domed Church near Addendan. From Geoffrey S. Mileham, *Churches in Lower Nubia*, US, University of Philadelphia, 1910.

prosperous and at the same time surprisingly free and egalitarian society, where differences in social status were not reflected in material culture.' Specifically concerning the village of Debeira West, Professors Oliver and Fagan report that: 'The University of Ghana ... [found that a]ll the buildings were of sun-dried brick, with vaulted ceilings. Two storeys were usual, with a stairway leading to the roof. The village shared a common sanitary and drainage system. There was a communal oil-press and an irrigation wheel.'

Old Dongola was the capital of the Empire of Makuria. From the seventh to ninth centuries AD, high status houses were built to the north of the ecclesiastical complex. Jakobielski provided further data on these houses: 'Further northwards extend a[n] ... eighth to ... ninth century housing complex. The houses discovered here differ in their hitherto unencountered spatial layout as well as their functional programme (water supply installation, bathroom with heating system) and interiors decorated with murals.'

Over the whole of this area churches and monasteries were found together with pottery kilns. Abu Salih wrote the following about the city: '[I]t is a large city on the banks of the blessed Nile, and contains many churches and large houses and wide streets. The king's house is lofty.'

The Throne Hall of the Kings was probably built in the ninth or tenth centuries AD. It was constructed almost exclusively of clay bricks with walls 1.1m thick. The ground floor consisted of long and narrow barrel-vaulted rooms of a lofty height. On entering the building, the doorway led to a monumental staircase winding around a square newel. On the first floor was a square hall, surrounded by an arcaded loggia on three sides and with additional rooms to the west, flanking the stairway. The Throne Hall had a timber roof supported by four columns.

Another writer, Ibn el-Faqih, writing around 900 AD, describes the city as encircled by seven walls, the lower parts of which were made of stone. At a later date, the earliest houses were demolished and replaced by newer houses of two storeys or more. Many of these houses still survive to a height of 3.7m with large arched windows in the upper storey or storeys. A feature of these houses, which is common to the houses excavated beyond the defences, is the presence of a narrow toilet unit by the external wall at the end of one room.

Soba was the capital of the Kingdom of Alwa. Of this city, Ibn Selim, an early visitor described 'fine buildings and large monasteries, churches rich with gold and gardens: there is also a great suburb where many Muslims live.' Its Throne Hall was a clay brick building 46.1m by 18.6m. It had long narrow rooms at ground floor level. Like the rooms in the Throne Hall at Old Dongola, its function was probably to elevate the palatial apartments. Archaeology has recovered fragments of ceramic grilles for windows. The window glass panes were also found close by. Evidence of window glass was also found at the Makurian cities of Old Dongola and Hambukol.

The West African Superstates

Ancient Ghana (in the period 700-1200 AD) dominated the same area as modern Mali and Mauritania. The power of the empire, at its height, even ruled the Senegal, Gambia and Guinea regions. Ghana's main cities were Nema, Walata, Audoghast and Kumbi-Saleh (the capital). Archaeological excavations of Kumbi-Saleh uncovered large houses (up to nine rooms) almost habitable today for want of renovation, several stories high with underground rooms, staircases and connecting halls. The masonry was

Figure 37. The Great Mosque of Djenné. Dedicated by Koi Konboro as a mosque in 1204 AD, it probably predates this as a palace. Although it has been rebuilt several times, always on the same plan, it gives a reasonable picture of 13th (or indeed 11th) century West African architecture. This is the largest clay brick building on earth. (Photo: Copyright Musée de l'Homme, Paris, Armée de l'Air).

excellent, with walls 30 cm thick. The Emperors of the twelfth century lived in a castle thoroughly fortified, with sculptures, paintings and glass windows. Kumbi-Saleh had a population several times greater than 30,000 people (cf. London's fourteenth century total of 20,000). Divided into two townships by religion, its suburbs had houses surrounded by gardens. Moreover, the non-Muslim part of the city had domed buildings indicating that domes were part of traditional non-Muslim architecture.

Mali, the successor empire, continued the architectural tradition but advanced it in the area of planning. It was common to find wide, straight thoroughfares lined on both sides by trees. In the fourteenth century, the great cities of Timbuktu, Djenné and Niani, its capital, dominated national life. The Hall of Audience, a Niani monument built by Mansa Musa I, was a building made of cut stone. It was surmounted by a dome and adorned with arabesques of striking colours. The windows of the upper floor were plated with wood and framed in silver foil. Those of the lower floor were plated with wood and framed in gold. Djenné was then an attractive eleven gated city, encircled by a rampart, with solid, well designed buildings of two stories. Among its many marvels was the Great Mosque, which remains a masterpiece of the Sudanic style of architecture.

Figure 38. There are bizarre and futuristic architectural pieces from this part of the world. The elegance of the domes and the spacing of the low relief chevron wall ornamentations show distinguished architectural and engineering skill. This village from Cameroon was photographed in 1912. No-one seems to know how old this architectural tradition was but it certainly predates the coming of the Europeans.

The West African Coastal States

The Yoruba Kingdom of Ife was located in southern Nigeria with Ile-Ife as its capital. Founded by the sixth century AD, by the twelfth century, the ruler lived in a palace made of enamelled brick and decorated with porcelain tiles. Ife's buildings were examples of impluvium architecture showing some similarities to the ancient city of Pompeii. Impluvium structures have four houses or sets of rooms at right angles to each other grouped around a single shared courtyard. The city had paved courtyards and public places decorated with Native American corncobs.

Susan Denyer detects a typical plan for Yoruba towns that echo the examples set by Ile-Ife and also Old Oyo. They had walls 4.5 metres high and had ditches cut around them. Ile-Ife had two concentric walls with ditches. Old Oyo was surrounded by a 25 km wall. At the centre of the city where two major roads intersected, lay the royal palace, itself enclosed by a clay wall, and next to it, the principal market. Another prominent feature was the temple or grove. The minor roads were divided into 'quarters' under the leadership of key dignitaries who exercised power and responsibility over the different heads of households. These 'quarters' were arranged around the royal palace in a satellite formation. The Yoruba palaces could have anything up to a hundred enormous courtyards, each far larger than that of an ordinary house. Their roofs were supported by elaborately carved wooden pillars inside and outside the building.

Great Benin (1460-1650) was located in southern Nigeria. The city houses were built in order, close to each other and lined the streets. As in Ife, the buildings were based on the impluvium idea, again showing some

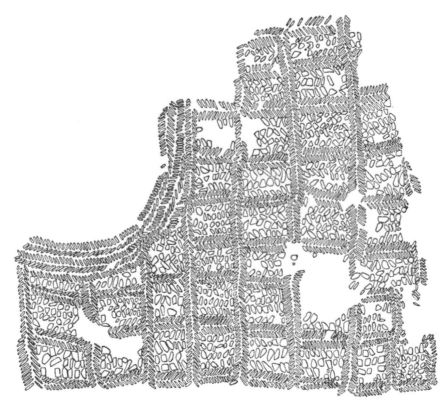

Figure 39. Sketch of an excavated Ile-Ife pavement from *c.*1000 AD by Susan Denyer showing chevron patterns forming squares with quartz pebbles set inside each square. American corncobs were used to make the chevron patterns.

similarities to the ancient city of Pompeii. Each house had many rooms with verandas, and often of two stories, some approached by steps. The walls were made of red clay. The roofs were made of banana leaves or palm. Moreover, all houses had wells supplying fresh water. The Kings Court was a city by itself and was comparable in size to whole European towns of that period. It could comfortably accommodate 15,000 people and had fluted walls and columns, some decorated with the famous Benin Bronze art. The city had perhaps 10,000 miles of walling and is reckoned by the *Guinness Book of Records* to have been the largest earthworks built by man in pre mechanical times. Benin City had a circumference of over 20 miles. It had 30 main roads, all 120 feet wide and very straight, laid out on a horizontal/vertical grid pattern. There were a large number of intersecting side streets.

Figure 40. One of the very many rooms inside the King's Court in Great Benin.

In the late eighteenth and early nineteenth century, Kumasi, the capital of the Ashanti Empire, now in modern day Ghana, was an impressive city. The houses were typically of two stories each containing a toilet on the second floor in a room by itself. The Royal Palace was particularly impressive. Built by local masons of Fanti origins, the building had ten courtyards, with a flat roof and parapet and contained a suite of apartments on the upper floor. A visitor to the palace remarked that they reminded him of Wardour Street in central London. Each room was a perfect Old Curiosity Shop.

The East African Coast

The East Coast, from Somalia to Mozambique, has ruins of well over 50 towns and cities. They flourished from the ninth to the sixteenth centuries due to their role in the Indian Ocean trade. One of these cities was Kilwa, a former seaport on the coast of Tanzania. In the fourteenth century, Kilwa was a very fine place. One visitor described it as 'one of the most beautiful and well-constructed cities in the world.' Basil Davidson says:

> Today, only a shabby village stands there. Yet beyond the village can still be found the walls and towers of ruined palaces and large houses and mosques, which is what the Moslems call their churches. A great palace [the Husuni Kubwa] has been dug out of the bushes that covered it for hundreds of years. It is a strange and beautiful ruin on a cliff over the Indian Ocean. Many other

ruins stand nearby. But the strangest thing about Kilwa and the other towns
nearby is that there is little to be found about them in the newer history books.
Even when the cities are described, they are said to be not African, but the work
of people from Arabia and Persia. History books saying this are out of date, and
they are wrong.

The other cities included the likes of Sinna, Zanzibar, Lamu, Mombasa,
Gedi and Mogadishu. Their mosques were 'as grand as the mediaeval
cathedrals of Europe'. The city of Lamu was apparently 'as sophisticated
as mediaeval Venice'. Tradition has it that Lamu, the best preserved of the
Swahili cities, was founded in 699 AD. Near its harbour are a number of
splendid mansions, now deserted. They have reception rooms whose walls
have tiered decorated niches. Also of interest is a fluted pillar tomb that
may date back to the fifteenth century period. The city has over 20
mosques, all whitewashed, and also a few palaces.

In Kilwa the ruined mosque was once the largest of the Swahili temples.
It was founded in the tenth or eleventh centuries AD, but it was enlarged in
the thirteenth and fifteenth centuries. The north prayer hall was built first.
It had a massive stone and concrete roof built on wooden rafters.
Supporting the roof were a series of nine wooden pillars of polygonal
shape. The domed extension, to the south, was built later. Between 1421
and 1430, it was rebuilt during the time of Sulaiman ibn Muhammad al-
Malik al-Adil. Its roof is a complicated construction and has barrel vaults
and domes over alternate bays. The interior has a forest of composite
octagonal columns of rubble and cut stone, set in mortar. To the south of
the mosque is a high wall that encloses an area for ablutions. It has water-
tanks, a well and stone slabs--on which feet were washed and dried. In
total, it was an admirable structure. One early Portuguese visitor compared
its domed ceiling to that of the Great Mosque of Cordova in Spain.

There are other buildings of historical interest in Kilwa. Located east of
the Husuni Kubwa is the Husuni Ndogo, a contemporaneous building
raised by al-Malik al-Mansur. The structure has a massive wall enclosing a
rectangular plan and covers an acre. At intervals along the walls and at the
corners, are solid towers. They are polygonal in shape but circular at the
base. The function of this great edifice is presently unknown but it may
have been a mosque or even a market. South and west of the Great Mosque,
lay the graveyard. This leads to a small domed fifteenth century temple. It
is the best preserved and ornamented of the old structures. The customary
vaults and domes ornament its roof, but an octagonal pillar, a most curious
feature, surmounts the central dome. Islamic ware, consisting of small

Figure 41. Ruins of the Royal Palace of Gedi in Kenya. Thirteenth century. (Photo: Robin Walker.)

bowls, was set into the ceilings of the vaults. Above the mihrab were recesses for tiles and bowls. The eastern side of the building has a room that may have functioned as a Koran school.

Gedi, near the coast of Kenya, is another ghost town. Its ruins, dating from the fourteenth or fifteenth centuries (the Kenyan museums say thirteenth), include the city walls, the palace, private houses, the Great Mosque, seven smaller mosques, and three pillar tombs. The walls are nine feet high and had at least three gates. Approaching the mosque was a washing pool for the believers to perform ablutions. It had a purifier made of limestone for recycling water. The houses had roofs of coral tiles covered in lime, walls of mortar and coral rag, and finely cut doorways of coral. The early houses were of one storey. They had a court, leading to the main room, and behind that was the private quarter. Also there, were smaller adjoining rooms, such as the bathroom, the toilet, bedroom, kitchen and storeroom. Later houses, from the fifteenth or sixteenth centuries, had upper floors. The royal palace had a layout similar to a large cluster of these houses, but with the addition of a reception hall. The palace contains evidence of bathrooms and indoor toilets. Finally, a part of this three-gated city had streets laid out on a north-south, east-west grid.

Southern Africa

In Southern Africa, there are at least 600 stone built ruins in the regions of Zimbabwe, Mozambique and South Africa. These ruins 'show today an extraordinary cultural past'. Most of them are said to date from the Middle Ages, but some authorities give much earlier dates for their construction. These structures are called Mazimbabwe in Shona, the Bantu language of the builders, and means great houses of stone. João de Barros, a Portuguese writer of the mid-sixteenth century, tells us 'Symbaoe' (more correctly 'Zimbabwe') in Shona 'signifies court'. Of the buildings themselves, Professor Diop informs us that:

> [T]hey are almost cyclopean structures, with walls several metres thick; five at the base, three at the top, and nine meters in height. Edifices of all types are to be found there from the royal palace, the temple, and the military fortification to the private villa of a notable. The walls are of granite masonry.

The Great Zimbabwe was the largest of these ruins. It consists of 12 clusters of buildings, spread over three square miles. Its outer walls were made from 100,000 tons of granite bricks. In the fourteenth century, the city housed 18,000 people (some give higher figures), comparable in size to that of London of the same period. The buildings housed warehouses and shrines.

The walls of the central enclosure, popularly known as the 'Temple', reach 35 feet in height and 17 feet thick in places. They form an irregular ellipse with a maximum diameter of 292 feet and a circumference of 830 feet. The bricks are fashioned and arranged to hold together in regular courses without the use of mortar. The floors are of crushed granite and contain drains. One of the earliest visitors to the site, J. Theodore Bent, commented that: 'As a specim[e]n of the dry builder's art, it is without a parallel.' The tops of some walls have ornamental patterns, of which chevron and dentelle are the most common. For over 250 feet of its length, the chevron pattern ornaments the outer wall and is perfectly level. On the summit of the wall above the chevron work, stood a series of granite and soapstone monoliths and also a double row of small granite towers. Some of the other ruins show check, sloping block, and herringbone patterns. The North Entrance has steps that curve inwards in a semicircular fashion. This

Figure 42. Great Zimbabwe Temple. *c*.1335 AD.

leads immediately inside to the great Parallel Passage, a distance of 220 feet.

Though succumbed to the passage of time, cottages once stood within and outside these walls for an area of three square miles. They were circular and thatched. Moreover, they had walls 12 to 18 inches thick and made of *daga,* a clay and gravel mixture. *Daga* was also used to make steps, fireplaces, chairs, bedsteads, and tables, all to a high level of smooth glazed finish. It was used to coat floors, again to a fine finish. Professor Finch notes that this must have had a 'dazzling' aesthetic effect.

The cottages were richly decorated with carved wooden beams and painted walls. Among the typical designs were paintings of animals, birds, people, and black and white squares. Some cottages had wooden doors, beautifully carved from selected timbers.

Perhaps the most well-known part of the ruined complex is the Conical Tower. The Parallel Passage leads on to this curious edifice. It is 18 feet in diameter at the base and 30 feet high, though once higher. Next to the tower is a much smaller cone structure. The Conical Tower may symbolise a mound of grain and therefore reinforce the role of the king as provider for the people.

On a hill 350 feet above and overlooking the Temple is a castle, generally known as the 'Acropolis'. It has very thick walls, massive conical turrets, narrow entrances, and twisting passageways. The widths of the entrances vary from half a metre to just over a metre. The widths of the walls vary from 12 to 14 feet at the top to 19 to 22 feet thick at the base. The site may well have been chosen for security reasons, giving a panoramic view of the city and the surroundings. What is interesting here is that the hill contains huge stone boulders. The builders incorporated the boulders into the walls rather than clearing them.

Ethiopia

In Ethiopia, in the Tigre region, stands the ruined Temple of Almaqah. The pride of the city of Yeha, it is one of the oldest monuments in the country. Some think it was built before 500 BC. The Temple is a two-storey structure, raised on a stepped plinth. It is 25 metres long and rectangular in plan. The walls are of huge limestone blocks, finely dressed and polished with two small windows.

In and around Axum, another great city, there are over 50 stelae, many of them undecorated. Some are believed to be very old, but firm dates have not been established. Near to some of these obelisks, one kilometre from Axum on the road to the city of Gondar, is a massive building containing a drainage system with 'finely-mortared stone walls, deep foundations and an impressive throne room'. Ethiopian tradition establishes this building as the palace of Empress Makeda, the fabled Queen of Sheba (1005-955 BC). Tradition also establishes one of the obelisks, carved with four horizontal bands, each topped with a row of circles in relief, as the marker of the Queen's grave.

Axum itself has a series of seven giant stelae that date from perhaps 300 BC to 300 AD (see frontispiece). They have details carved into them that represent windows and doorways of several storeys. The largest obelisk, now fallen, is in fact 'the largest monolith ever made anywhere in the world'. It is 108 feet long, weighs a staggering 500 tons, and represents a 13 storey building. The largest standing obelisk is 75 feet tall and represents a nine-storey building.

The Maryam Seyon is Ethiopia's most important church. It is one of the oldest cathedrals in the world. The foundations of the Maryam Seyon were established in 340 AD during the time of King Ezana. However, a smaller seventeenth-century church with the same name was built next to this site by Emperor Fasilides. The contemporary Cathedral of Our Lady St Mary of Zion, built in the 1950s, also stands on the same site. The importance of the site is augmented by the belief that the Ark of the Covenant is housed in a nearby building. Concerning the foundation of the original fourth century building, Francisco Alvarez, a Portuguese visitor to Ethiopia in the 1520s, repeated the local legend.

[N]ow the foundation was performed by means of a miracle, for previously

Figure 43. Temple of Yeha. Built before 500 BC. (Photo: Louis Buckley of Black Nine Films.)

> there was (there) a great lake; and the holy kings ... climbed a great mountain
> called Mekyada Egziena and prayed that (God) might reveal to them where
> they should build a cathedral for the dwelling-place of His name. And Our Lord
> descended and stood between them, and took earth, and cast it where it is now;
> and above (the place) there stood a column of light; and there they built the
> sanctuary; and behold it is there to this day.

Beta Samati is an ancient, ruined town that is adding to our understanding of Axumite history. Beta Samati means 'house of audience' in Ethiopia's Tigrinya tongue. Located 30 miles northeast of Aksum, the remains of a 1700-year-old church were found there. It was 60 foot by 40 foot and dates back to the time when Ethiopia adopted Christianity during the reign of King Ezana.

The Tigray region in northern Ethiopia has more than 100 rock-hewn monolithic churches. These structures were chiselled by hand into mountains and cliffs in the 5th and 6th centuries AD. Many are still used during Ethiopia's religious festivals. Named after father Yemata, the Abuna Yemata Church is one of the most inaccessible in the world. This is a 5th century monolithic church set in a cliff to an astonishing height of 8,640 feet (2,580 meters). It is aptly named the chapel in the sky. The Debre Damo Monastery is one of the main centres of Christianity in Ethiopia. It is named after its founder, Abuna Za-Mikael, one of the nine saints credited with spreading Christianity throughout the land. It is located on a 3000-meter hill in the Tigray region. The legend says that he climbed to the top of the flat-topped mountain on the back of a python. In observance to this miracle, visitors to this monastery must climb 15 meters on a vertical rock face by a plaited leather rope.

In the western highlands of Ethiopia, approximately 400 miles from Addis Ababa, at an altitude of around 2000m lays the town of Lalibela. The town was named after King Gebre Mesquel Lalibela, who was the Emperor of Ethiopia of the Zagwe dynasty from 1181 to 1221. Legend says, King Lalibela had a vision; to create a New Jerusalem since Islamic conquests made Christian pilgrimage to the holy land unfeasible. In the 1520s, Portuguese priest Francisco Alvarez travelled to Ethiopia and chronicled what he witnessed. He wrote 'First he (Lalibela) made a church like that which God had shown him, of beautiful work, and with beautiful art, which is impossible to achieve, but through the wisdom of God'. King Lalibela commissioned a complex of 11 unique churches that were sculpted from the living rock. The 800-year-old churches are still used as places of worship and pilgrimage.

The monolithic blocks were chiselled by hand to form windows, doors, and roofs. The churches are connected by a network of underground passages and aisles. They are arranged into two groups: One group of churches represents Jerusalem on earth, the other group represent heavenly Jerusalem. In between the groups of churches is a trench that represents the River Jordan. Describing the distinctiveness of the Lalibela complex, Francisco Alvarez writes; 'At a day's journey from this Church of Imbra Christo are buildings, the like of which and so many cannot, as it appears to me, be found in the world, and they are churches entirely excavated in the (living, soft) rock (or tufa), very well hewn. The names of these churches are these: Emmanuel, St Saviour, St Mary, Holy Cross, St George, Golgotha, Bethlehem, Marcoreos, the Martyrs. The principle one is Lalibela'. All the temples were carved to a depth of 11 metres or so below ground level.

The largest is the House (or Church) of the Redeemer, a staggering 33.7 metres long, 23.7 metres wide and 11.5 metres deep. It is entirely surrounded by a forest of columns, all carved and sculpted. It is one of four churches that give the illusion of being freestanding, connected only by their bases to the rock from which they were hewn.

The House of Mary is another of the 'freestanding' churches. The Emperor considered it one of his favourites and the royal family used it to hold mass. It is 15 metres long, 11 metres wide and 10 metres deep. In its courtyard is a deep square baptismal pool.

Perhaps the most celebrated of the Lalibela churches is the House of Saint George. From the top of the monument, looking downwards, the church is in the shape of a concentric cross. It is more than 12 metres deep and its outer wall seem to indicate four storeys. Like the Temple of Almaqah, the church was built on a podium. The bottom rows of windows are similar in design to those seen on the old Axum monoliths. Other windows have pointed arches.

The architects of Lalibela seem to have absorbed or developed a wide range of styles. The House of Golgotha has pointed arch windows, with a tendrille-like tracery topped by a cross, similar to a Maltese cross. The House of Abba Libanos has plain pointed arch windows but also cross-shaped openings. The House of Mascal has Romanesque arches and windows of twinned crosses. The House of Mary has swastika-shaped windows.

After describing the spectacular churches in Lalibela, Francisco Alvarez wrote:

Figure 44. House of Saint George. This is the most celebrated of the 11 Lalibela churches (1181 to 1221 AD). Like the other churches, this was carved out of the rock of the mountains by hammer and chisel.

I weary of writing more about these buildings, because it seems to me that I shall not be believed if I write more, and because regarding what I have already written they may blame me for untruth, therefore I swear by God, in Whose power I am, that all that I have written is the truth (to which nothing has been added), and there is much more than what I have written, and I have left it that they may not tax me with its being falsehood (show great was my desire to make known this splendour to the world).

The sight of Lalibela at the pinnacle of its splendour must have been astounding. The churches of Lalibela are a marvel of world architecture and are deemed to be the Eighth Wonder of the World. UNESCO has listed the churches as a world heritage site. The sentiments expressed in the 15th century by Francisco Alvarez were augmented in the 21st century by a journalist called Jack Barker. He wrote, "I have always questioned God's existence, but in the northern Ethiopian town of Lalibela, I was presented with fairly substantial evidence".

To give some idea of the technological effort involved, Bernhard Lindahl of The Nordic African Institute says: 'An estimate of excavation volumes gave as result that for three churches Maryam, Amanuel and Giyorgis it was over 107,000 cubic metres, that is to say five times the volume for Abu Simbel in Egypt.'

Lalibela is not the only place to have such wonders. Peter Garlake, author of *Early Art and Architecture of Africa,* reports research that was conducted in the region in the early 1970s when: 'startling numbers of churches built in caves or partially or completely cut from the living rock were revealed not only in Tigre and Lalibela but as far south as Addis Ababa. Soon at least 1,500 were known. At least as many more probably await revelation to the outside world. A whole realm of architectural history awaits recording, study, and understanding.'

In the seventeenth century, Gondar, became the new capital. Emperor Fasilides founded the city and adorned it with huge gardens complete with pools and zoological collections. He built several schools and churches and aimed for the city to become a great place of commerce. Gondar has, however, been dubbed 'the Camelot of Africa' in reference to the fairytale castles that adorn its centre.

The oldest of the castles is said to have been constructed in around 1640 by an Indian architect. No such foreign claims have been made about the other buildings, however. These include the castle built during the time of Emperor Yohannes I (1667-1682) which functioned as a library. There is another famous castle, now derelict, built by Iyasu the Great (1682-1706). The Library was a two storey cuboidal building that had a parapeted flat

Figure 45. Archive (far left) and Library (centre) at Gondar. Both built by Emperor Yohannes I (1667-1682 AD). Castle (far right) built by Emperor Bakaffa (1721-1730 AD). (Photo: Louis Buckley, Black Nine Films.)

roof and an outside staircase. The derelict building, sometimes called the Archive, in its time was ornamented with paintings, mirrors and ivory. Gold leaf and precious stones adorned its ceiling. Also in the royal compound is the Palace of Mentuwab, the Castle of King David, and the Banqueting Hall of Emperor Bakaffa. Surrounding the Royal Compound is a 900-metre-long wall with twelve gated towers and three bridges. Fasilides' bath is located outside of the centre of Gondar. The edifice includes a three-storied palace and a square pool. The palace is connected to the ground by a bridge with stone arches which could be moved during times of conflict. This stunning palace has been used in Timkat festivals for over three hundred years. This festival celebrates the baptism of Jesus in the River Jordan. The Gondar region represents some of Ethiopia's finest classical architecture and serves as a reminder of Africa's advanced indigenous civilizations. The royal palace complex is registered as one of UNESCOs world heritage sites.

BIBLIOGRAPHY

PREFACE BY THE FORMER PRIME MINISTER OF ETHIOPIA, HIS EXCELLENCY, MR HAILEMARIAM DESALEGN

Benaebi Benatari, *The Document of African Civilisation,* UK, Unpublished Paper, 1995, p. 16

Basil Davidson editor, *African Civilization Revisited,* US, Africa World Press, 1991, pp. 31-32

P. Diagne, *History and Linguistics* in *UNESCO General History of Africa, Volume 1,* edited by J. Ki-Zerbo, UK, Heinemann, 1981, pp. 250-252

Cheikh Anta Diop, *Precolonial Black Africa,* US, Lawrence Hill, 1987, pp. 188-189

Dag Herbjørnsrud, *The African Enlightenment,* in *Aeon,* see website aeon.co, 13 December 2017

Updated from Keith C. Holmes, *Black Inventors: Crafting Over 200 Years of Success,* US, Global Black Inventor Research Projects, 2008, pp. 32, 37, 57, 59, 60, 79, 102, 105, 125

John O. Hunwick & Alida Jay Boye, *The Hidden Treasures of Timbuktu: Historic City of Islamic Africa,* UK, Thames & Hudson, 2008, pp. 95-97

Y. M. Kobishanov, *Aksum: political system, economics and culture, first to fourth century,* in *UNESCO General History of Africa. Volume 2,* editor G. Mokhtar, US, Heinemann, 1981, pp. 381-399

Saki Mafundikwa, *Afrikan Alphabets,* US, Mark Batty, 2004, pp. 51-93

Momolu Massaquoi, *The Vai people and their syllabic writing,* in *Journal of the African Society, Volume X, Number XL,* July 1911, pp. 459-466 and plates

Chris Rainier, *Reclaiming the Ancient Manuscripts of Timbuktu*, in *National Geographic*, 27 May 2003

Laura Roberts, *Manuscript found in Ethiopian monastery could be world's oldest illustrated Christian work*, in *The Telegraph*, 5 July 2010

INTRODUCTION

Duncan MacNaughton, *A Scheme of Egyptian Chronology*, UK, Luzac & Co., 1932, pp. 12-26

G. Mokhtar, *Annex to Chapter 1: Report of the symposium on The Peopling of Ancient Egypt and the Deciphering of the Meroitic Script*, in *UNESCO General History of Africa, Volume 2*, UK, James Currey, 1990, pp. 35, 37, 55

W. M. Flinders Petrie, *Researches in Sinai*, UK, John Murray, 1906, pp. 163-185

André Pochan, *L'Enigme de la Grande Pyramide*, France, Éditions Robert Laffont, 1971, pp. 309-315.

Gay Robins and C. C. D. Shute, *The Physical Proportions and Living Stature of New Kingdom Pharaohs*, in *Journal of Human Biology, Volume 12*, 1983, pp. 455, 461

Robin Walker, *When We Ruled, 2nd Edition*, UK, Reklaw Education Ltd, 2013, pp. 277-316

CHAPTER 1 METALLURGY

Metallurgy in Ancient Egypt

Charles S. Finch, *The Star of Deep Beginnings*, US, Khenti, 1998, pp. 28-30, 35-38, 48

Metallurgy in West Africa

Fred Anozie, *Metal Technology in Precolonial Nigeria*, in *African Systems of Art, Science and Technology*, edited by Gloria Thomas-Emeagwali, UK, Karnak House, 1993, pp. 83, 89

Georges Balandier, *Daily Life in the Kingdom of Kongo,* UK, George Allen and Unwin, 1968, pp. 112-113

Benaebi Benatari, *The Document of African Civilisation,* UK, Unpublished Paper, 1995, pp. 18-19

Cheikh Anta Diop, *Precolonial Black Africa,* US, Lawrence Hill, 1987, pp. 116-117, 204

Charles S. Finch, *The Star of Deep Beginnings,* US, Khenti, 1998, pp. 32-33, 43, 45-47, 48, 52-53, colour plates 3 and 4

Ekpo Eyo and Frank Willett, *Treasures of Ancient Nigeria,* UK, William Collins & Sons, 1980, pp. 148-149

Lady Lugard, *A Tropical Dependency,* UK, James Nisbet & Co., 1906, pp. 99, 112 and 208

Laure Mayer, *Black Africa: Masks, Sculpture, Jewelry,* France, Éditions Pierre Terrail, 1992, p. 179

Sir Herbert Richmond Palmer, *The Bornu Sahara and Sudan,* UK, John Murray, 1936, frontispiece

Amon Sakaana & Adetokunbo Pearse, *Towards the Decolonization of the British Educational System,* UK, Karnak House, 1986, p. 114

Fari Supiya, *Afterword: Where From Here?* in *When We Ruled, 2nd Edition,* by Robin Walker, UK, Reklaw Education, 2013, pp. 752-755

Robin Walker, *Before The Slave Trade,* UK, Black History Studies, 2008, pp. 6-7

Metallurgy in Kush also East and South Africa

J. Theodore Bent, *The Ruined Cities of Mashonaland, 3rd Edition,* UK, Longmans, Green, and Co., 1902, p. 308

Ian D. Colvin, *Zimbabwe's Ruins of Mystery,* in *Wonders of the Past, Volume 2,* editor Sir J. A. Hammerton, UK, Amalgamated Press, 1937, p. 969

Charles Finch, *The Star of Deep Beginnings,* US, Khenti, 1998, pp. 28, 30-32, 38-47, 50-51

Peter Garlake, *Early Art and Architecture of Africa,* UK, Oxford University Press, 2002, p. 84

Peter Garlake, *The Kingdoms of Africa,* UK, Elsevier Phaidon, 1978, pp. 78-79

A. A. Hakem, *The civilization of Napata and Meroe,* in *UNESCO General History of Africa, Volume 2,* edited by G. Mokhtar, UK, James Currey, 1990, p. 311

Roland Oliver and Brian Fagan, *Africa in the Iron Age,* UK, Cambridge University Press, 1975, p. 109

Debra Shore, *Steel-Making in Ancient Africa,* in *Blacks in Science: Ancient and Modern,* edited by Ivan Van Sertima, US, Transaction Publishers, 1983, pp. 157-162

Dietrich Wildung, *The Treasure of Amanishakheto,* in *Sudan: Ancient Kingdoms of the Nile,* edited by Dietrich Wildung, France, The Institut du monde arabe, 1997, pp. 301-340

Metallurgy in Ethiopia

David Buxton, *The Abyssinians,* UK, Thames and Hudson, 1970, pp. 36-37, 162-177

Charles Finch, *The Star of Deep Beginnings,* US, Khenti, 1998, pp. 31-32, 45, 50

Belai Giday, *Ethiopian Civilization,* Ethiopia, Belai Giday, 1988, pp. 61-69, 92

Roderick Grierson editor, *African Zion: The Sacred Art of Ethiopia,* US, Yale University Press, 1993, pp. 101-113

Stuart Munro-Hay, *Aksum An African Civilization of Late Antiquity,* UK, 1991, pp. 150-165

The British Museum, *Aksumite Coins,* see https://smarthistory.org/aksumite-coins/

CHAPTER 2 MATHEMATICS

Mathematics in Ancient Egypt

Cheikh Anta Diop, *Civilization or Barbarism,* US, Lawrence Hill Books, 1991, pp. 231-278

Charles S. Finch, *The Star of Deep Beginnings,* US, Khenti, 1998, pp. 57-91

Beatrice Lumpkin, *Mathematics and Engineering in the Nile Valley,* in *Egypt: Child of Africa,* edited by Ivan Van Sertima, US, Transaction Publishers, 1994, pp. 323-340

Theophile Obenga, *African Philosophy: The Pharaonic Period: 2780-330 BC,* Senegal, Per Ankh, 2004, pp. 421-498

Claudia Zaslavsky, *The Yoruba Number System,* in *Blacks in Science: Ancient and Modern,* edited by Ivan Van Sertima, US, Transaction Publishers, 1983, pp. 113-116

Mathematics in Yoruba, West Africa, Benin and Congo

Curtis Abraham, *Stars of the Sahara,* in *New Scientist, Issue 2617,* 15 August 2007, pp. 39-41

Ron Eglash, *African Fractals,* US, Rutgers University Press, 1999, pp. 20-33

Charles S. Finch, *The Star of Deep Beginnings,* US, Khenti, 1998, pp. 91-94

Henry Louis Gates, *Into Africa,* Television Series Part 5, *The Road To Timbuktu,* UK, BBC Television, 1999

John O. Hunwick & Alida Jay Boye, *The Hidden Treasures of Timbuktu: Historic City of Islamic Africa,* UK, Thames & Hudson, 2008, p. 90

Karen E. Lange, *Djénné: West Africa's Eternal City,* in *National Geographic,* US, June 2001, p. 110

Beatrice Lumpkin, *African & African-American Contributions to Mathematics,* US, Portland Public Schools, 1987, pp. 40-41

Claudia Zaslavsky, *Africa Counts,* US, Lawrence Hill, 1973, pp. 105-107, 137-151, 190-193, 204-210, 213-218

Mathematics in Mozambique, etcetera

Paulus Gerdes, *Geometry From Africa,* US, The Mathematical Association of America, 1999, pp. 89-125

Mathematics in Ethiopia

Otto Neugebauer, *Chronography in Ethiopic Sources,* Germany, Osterreiche Akademie Der Wissenschaften, 1989, pp. 27-30

Otto Neugebauer, *Ethiopic Astronomy and Computus,* Germany, Osterreiche Akademie Der Wissenschaften, 1979, pp. 7-10, 13-17, 18, 27-66, 111, 123-124, 132, 175-177, 221-222

David Okuefuna (Executive Producer), *Go Forth and Multiply,* UK, The Open University for BBC 4, Television Programme, 2005

CHAPTER 3 ASTRONOMY

Astronomy in Ancient Egypt

Cheikh Anta Diop, *Civilization or Barbarism,* US, Lawrence Hill Books, 1991, pp. 278-282

Charles S. Finch, *The Star of Deep Beginnings,* US, Khenti, 1998, pp. 167-195

George R. Goodman, *The Age of Unreason,* in *The Freethinker, Volume 85,* London, 1965, p. 182

Duncan MacNaughton, *A Scheme of Egyptian Chronology,* UK, Luzac & Co., 1932, pp. 110, 236 and plates III, VII, VIII, X, XI, XII and XIII

Theophile Obenga, *African Philosophy: The Pharaonic Period: 2780-330 BC,* Senegal, Per Ankh, 2004, pp. 91-118, 134-146 and 343-344

John Pappademos, *The Newtonian Synthesis in Physical Science and its roots in the Nile Valley*, in *Egypt: Child of Africa*, edited by Ivan Van Sertima, US, Transaction Publishers, 1994, pp. 305-322

Astronomy in West Africa

Curtis Abraham, *Stars of the Sahara*, in *New Scientist, Issue 2617*, 15 August 2007, pp. 39-41

Hunter Havelin Adams III, *African & African-American Contributions to Science and Technology*, US, Portland Public Schools, 1987, p. 60

Hunter Havelin Adams III, *African Observers of the Universe: The Sirius Question*, in *Blacks in Science: Ancient and Modern*, edited by Ivan Van Sertima, US, Transaction Publishers, 1983, pp. 27-46

Hunter Havelin Adams III, *New Light on the Dogon and Sirius*, in *Blacks in Science: Ancient and Modern*, edited by Ivan Van Sertima, US, Transaction Publishers, 1983, pp. 47-50

Charles S. Finch, *The Star of Deep Beginnings*, US, Khenti, 1998, pp. 235-260

Marcel Griaule & Germaine Dieterlen, *The Pale Fox*, US, Continuum Foundation, 1986, pp. 193-194, 201, 423, 445 and 505

Sharron Hawkes (producer), *The Ancient Astronomers of Timbuktu*, DVD, 2009

Michael Palin, *Sahara*, Television Series Part 3: *Absolute Desert*, UK, BBC Worldwide Limited, 2002

Astronomy in East and South Africa

Demissew Bekele, *A Glimpse of Ancient Ethiopian Astronomy*, 3 July 2011, online pdf, pp. 23-25

Cheikh Anta Diop, *Precolonial Black Africa*, US, Lawrence Hill Books, 1987, pp. 196-198

Laurance R. Doyle, *Astronomy of Africa,* in *Encyclopaedia of the History of Science, Technology and Medicine in Non-Western Cultures.* See internet at http://www.safaris.cc/8art.encyclo.htm.

Charles Finch, *The Star of Deep Beginnings,* US, Khenti, 1998, pp. 168-169, 195-198

John G. Jackson, *Ethiopia and the Origin of Civilization,* US, Black Classic Press Reprint, original 1939, pp. 12-16

Lucian is quoted in John G. Jackson, 1939

Lady Lugard, *A Tropical Dependency,* UK, James Nisbet & Co., 1906, p. 220

Roland Oliver and Brian M. Fagan, *Africa in the Iron Age,* UK, Cambridge University Press, 1975, p. 208

Ivan Van Sertima editor, *Blacks in Science: Ancient and Modern,* US, Transaction Publishers, 1983, pp. 10, 51-56

Count De Volney is quoted in John G. Jackson, 1939

Derek A. Welsby, *The Medieval Kingdoms of Nubia,* UK, The British Museum Press, 2002, p. 62

Astronomy in Ethiopia

Asmarom Legesse, *Gada: Three Approaches to the Study of African Society,* US, The Free Press, 1973, pp. 177, 180-182

Otto Neugebauer, *Ethiopic Astronomy and Computus,* Germany, Osterreiche Akademie Der Wissenschaften, 1979, pp. 7-8, 13-14, 18, 20, 91, 95, 99, 107-108, 183-184, 198, 200-201, 227, 232-233

Space in Africa, *Ethiopia given naming rights to some celestial bodies by International Astronomical Union,* see http://africanews.space/Ethiopia-given-naming-rights-to-some-celestial-bodies-by-international-astronomical-union/, 23 May 2019

CHAPTER 4 MEDICINE AND SURGERY

Medicine in Ancient Egypt

Hunter Havelin Adams III, *African & African-American Contributions to Science and Technology,* US, Portland Baseline Essay, 1986, pp. 45-48 and Figures 25 and 26

Cheikh Anta Diop, *Civilization or Barbarism,* US, Lawrence Hill Books, 1991, pp. 283-284

Charles S. Finch, *Africa and the birth of science and technology: A brief overview,* US, Khenti, 1992, pp. 13-17

Charles S. Finch, *Science and Symbol in Egyptian Medicine: Commentaries on the Edwin Smith Papyrus,* in *Egypt Revisited,* edited by Ivan Van Sertima, US, Transaction Publishers, 1989, pp. 325-351

Charles S. Finch, *The African Background of Medical Science,* in *Blacks in Science: Ancient and Modern,* edited by Ivan Van Sertima, US, Transaction Publishers, 1983, pp. 140-147

Frederick Newsome, *Black Contributions to the Early History of Medicine,* from *Blacks in Science: Ancient and Modern,* edited by Ivan Van Sertima, US, Transaction Publishers, 1983, pp. 127-139

Théophile Obenga, *African Philosophy: The Pharaonic Period: 2780-330 BC,* Senegal, Per Ankh, 2004, pp. 371-381, 400, 412-414, 418-420

Medicine and Surgery in West Africa

Benaebi Benatari, *The Document of African Civilisation,* UK, Unpublished Paper, 1995, p. 19

Basil Davidson, *African Kingdoms,* Netherlands, Time-Life Books, 1967, p. 85

Cheikh Anta Diop, *Precolonial Black Africa,* US, Lawrence Hill, 1987, pp. 205-206 and 227

Charles S. Finch, *Africa and the Birth of Science and Technology*, US, Khenti, 1992, pp. 26-28

Charles S. Finch, *The African Background of Medical Science*, in *Blacks in Science: Ancient and Modern*, edited by Ivan Van Sertima, US, Transaction Publishers, 1983, p. 150

Aminatta Forma (presenter), *The Lost Libraries of Timbuktu*, Television Programme, UK, BBC Television, 2009

Eugenia Herbert, *Smallpox Inoculation in Africa*, in *Journal of African History, Volume 16: No. 4*, UK, Cambridge University Press, 1975, pp. 539-559

Time-Life Books, *Africa's Glorious Legacy*, US, Time-Life Books Inc., 1994, p. 85

Medicine and Surgery in East and South Africa

A. T. Bryant, *Zulu Medicine and Medicine-Men*, South Africa, Centaur Publishers, 1966, pp. Inside cover note, 7, 10, 11, 13, 15-16, 19-20, 22-23, 86-115

Charles S. Finch, *The African Background of Medical Science*, in *Blacks in Science: Ancient and Modern*, edited by Ivan Van Sertima, US, Transaction Publishers, 1983, pp. 151-153 and 155

Charles S. Finch, *Africa and the Birth of Science and Technology*, US, Khenti, 1992, pp. 25-26, 29-32 and 39

Medicine and Surgery in Ethiopia and Somalia

Richard Pankhurst, *An Introduction to the Medical History of Ethiopia*, US, Red Sea Press, 1990, pp. 26-30, 75-80, 93-101, 104-111, 113-136

CHAPTER 5 ARCHITECTURE

Architecture in Ancient Egypt

Nnamdi Elleh, *African Architecture: Evolution and Transformation*, US, McGraw-Hill, 1997, pp. 22-41

Charles S. Finch, *The Star of Deep Beginnings,* US, Khenti, 1998, pp. 101-135

Dietrich Wildung, *Egypt from Prehistory to the Romans,* Germany, Taschen, 1997, pp. 7-165

Architecture in West Africa

Benaebi Benatari, *The Document of African Civilisation,* UK, Unpublished Paper, 1995, pp. 15 and 17-18

Thomas Bowditch, *At Kumasi,* in *African Civilization Revisited,* edited by Basil Davidson, US, Africa World Press, 1991, p. 385

Susan Denyer, *African Traditional Architecture,* UK, Heinemann, 1978, pp. 33, 35-36, 56, 71, 80, 82, 87, 90, 121

Cheikh Anta Diop, *Precolonial Black Africa,* US, Lawrence Hill, 1987, pp. 83-84, 199-203

Nnamdi Elleh, *African Architecture: Evolution and Transformation,* US, McGraw Hill, 1997, pp. 25, 306-309

Norris & Ross McWhirter, *Guinness Book of Records, 21st Edition,* UK, Guinness Superlatives Limited, October 1974, p. 129

H. Ling Roth, *Great Benin: Its Customs, Art and Horrors,* UK, F. King and Sons, 1903, pp. 160-161

Reade, *The Palace, Kumasi, 1874* in *Pageant of Ghana,* edited by Freda Wolfson, UK, Oxford University Press, 1958, pp. 161-162

Architecture in East and South Africa

J. Theodore Bent, *The Ruined Cities of Mashonaland, 3rd Edition,* UK, Longmans, Green, and Co., 1902, pp. 110-111

Charles Bonnet, *The Kingdom of Kerma,* in *Sudan: Ancient Kingdoms of the Nile,* edited by Dietrich Wildung, France, The Institut du monde arabe, 1997, pp. 89-90

John Lewis Burckhardt, *Travels in Nubia,* UK, John Murray, 1819, p. 500

Vivian Davies and Renée Friedman, *Egypt,* UK, British Museum Press, 1998, pp. 103-107, 122-129

João de Barros, *Mines and Fortresses,* in *African Civilization Revisited,* edited by Basil Davidson, US, Africa World Press, 1991, p. 182

H. N. Chittick, *A Guide to the Ruins of Kilwa,* Tanzania, Ministry of Community Development and Culture, 1965, whole booklet

Basil Davidson, *A Guide to African History,* US, Zenith Books, 1965, pp. 30-32

Cheikh Anta Diop, *Precolonial Black Africa,* US, Lawrence Hill Books, 1987, pp. 196-197

David Dugan, *Time Life's Lost Civilizations,* video series, *Africa, A History Denied,* Holland, Time Life Video, 1995

Nnamdi Elleh, *African Architecture: Evolution and Transformation,* US, McGraw-Hill, 1997, pp. 44-46, 133-137, 149, 165-166, 209-214

Charles Finch, *The Star of Deep Beginnings,* US, Khenti, 1998, pp. 142-160

Peter Garlake, *Early Art and Architecture of Africa,* UK, Oxford University Press, 2002, pp. 54-63, 67-68, 75-84, 88-92, 171-184

S. Jakobielski, *Christian Nubia at the height of its civilization,* in *UNESCO General History of Africa: Volume 3,* editor M. Al Fasi, UK, Heinemann, 1988, pp. 200-204

Ronald Lewcock, *Zanj, the East African Coast,* in *Shelter in Africa,* editor Paul Oliver, UK, Barrie & Jenkins, 1971, pp. 80-87

Geoffrey S. Mileham, *Churches in Lower Nubia,* US, University of Philadelphia, 1910, whole book

Roland Oliver and Brian M. Fagan, *Africa in the Iron Age,* UK, Cambridge University Press, 1975, p. 125

P. L. Shinnie and M. Shinnie, *New Light on Medieval Nubia,* in *Papers in African Prehistory,* editors J. D. Fage and R. A. Oliver, UK, Cambridge University Press, 1970, pp. 283-284

F. M. C. Stokes, *Zimbabwe,* in *The Geographical Magazine, Volume II: No.2,* edited by Michael Huxley, UK, The Geographical Magazine, December 1935, pp. 143-153

Derek A. Welsby, *The Medieval Kingdoms of Nubia,* UK, The British Museum Press, 2002, whole book

Dietrich Wildung, *Egypt from Prehistory to the Romans,* Germany, Taschen, 1997, pp. 42-43, 180-189

Chancellor Williams, *The Destruction of Black Civilization,* US, Third World Press, 1987, pp. 149-151

Architecture in Ethiopia

Francisco Alvarez is quoted in C. F. Beckingham and G. W. B. Huntingford editors, *The Prester John of The Indies, Volume II,* UK, Published for The Hakluyt Society by Cambridge University Press, 1961

Jack Barker, *Ethiopia's miraculous underground churches,* see https://www.bbc.co.uk/travel/article/20170817-ethiopias-miraculous-underground-churches, 19 August 2017

Camerapix, *Ethiopia: A Tourist Paradise,* Ethiopia, Ethiopian Tourist Commission, 1996, whole book

Mary Anne Fitzgerald and Phillip Marsden, *Ethiopia The Living Churches of an Ancient Kingdom,* Egypt, The American University in Cairo Press, 2017

Graham Hancock, *The Beauty of Historic Ethiopia,* Kenya, Camerapix, 1996, whole book

Dr Lawrence E. Henry, *Ethiopia: Saving Christianity for the Kingdom of Heaven: The Untold Story,* US, Christian Faith Publishing, 2020

Trevor Jenner, *Ethiopia: Travellers' Handbook,* US, Trans-Atlantic Publications, Inc., 2016

Andrew Lawler, *Church Unearthed in Ethiopia Rewrites the History of Christianity in Africa,* see https://www.smithsonianmag.com/history/church-unearthed-ethiopia-rewrites-history-christianity-africa-180973740/, 10 December 2019

Bernhard Lindahl, *Lalibela,* in *Local History of Ethiopia,* see https://nai.uu.se/download/18.39fca04516faedec8b248e0f/1580829012921/O RTLAL05.pdf, The Nordic Africa Institute, 2005

Kristen Windmuller-Luna, *Monumental Architecture and Stelae of the Aksumite Empire,* US, The Metropolitan Museum of Art, 2000

PART TWO

ABOUT THE AUTHORS

ABOUT THE AUTHORS

Robin Walker 'The Black History Man'

Robin Walker 'The Black History Man' was born in London but has also lived in Jamaica. He attended the London School of Economics and Political Science where he read Economics.

In 1991 and 1992, he studied African World Studies with the brilliant Dr Femi Biko and later with Mr Kenny Bakie. Between 1993 and 1994, he trained as a secondary school teacher at Edge Hill College (linked to the University of Lancaster).

Since 1992 and up to the present period, Robin Walker has lectured in adult education, taught university short courses, and chaired conferences in African World Studies, Egyptology and Black History. The venues have been in Toxteth (Liverpool), Manchester, Leeds, Bradford, Huddersfield, Birmingham, Cambridge, Buckinghamshire and London.

Since 1994 he has taught Economics, Business & Finance, Mathematics, Information Communications Technology, PSHE/Citizenship and also History at various schools in London and Essex.

In 2006 he wrote the seminal *When We Ruled*. It is the most advanced synthesis on Ancient and Mediaeval African history ever written by a single author. It established his reputation as the leading Black History educational service provider. In 2011 Black Classic Press of Baltimore published a US version of this book.

Between 2013 and 2020, he followed this with *When We Ruled: Second Edition, When We Ruled Study Guide and Reading Plan, Blacks and Science Volumes I, II and III, Blacks and Religion Volumes I and II, The Rise and Fall of Black Wall Street and the Seven Key Empowerment Lessons, The Black Musical Tradition and Early Black Literature, 19 Lessons in Black History* and *Black History Matters*.

He also wrote four books in collaboration with others: *Everyday Life in an Early West African Empire, African Mathematics: History, Study Guide and Classroom Lessons, Black British History: Black Influences on British Culture 1948-2016* and *30 Black History Icons*.

John Matthews

John Matthews was born and raised in London. He attended Greenwich University where he read Accounting and Finance. He is a personal mathematics tutor with over 20 years of experience. He has taught mathematics at one of London's finest institutes of Higher Education. He has also taught at one of London's most recognised Supplementary Schools. He co-wrote the book: *African Mathematics: History, Study Guide and Classroom Lessons.*

He enjoys using his abundant gifts to empower and motivate learners to activate their hidden mathematical genius.

Speaking Engagements

Looking for a speaker for your next event?

Robin Walker 'The Black History Man' is dynamic and engaging, both as a speaker and a workshop leader. He brings Black or African history alive, making it relevant for the present generation. You will love his perfect blend of accessibility, engagement, and academic rigour where learning becomes fun. He has a lecture called *The African Origin of Mathematics.* Motivational crowds, general audiences, schools and parents will also enjoy his highly engaging presentation *Sub Saharan Africa in the Mainstream of Science History.*

John Matthews is engaging, dynamic and enthusiastic as a tutor and as a public speaker. He can make mathematics both relevant and fun with his unique delivery. Both adult and child learners have all benefitted from John's special talents. He gives lectures to a variety of audiences.

Adults and child learners will be empowered by the lecture called *The Keys To Unlocking Your Hidden Mathematical Genius* and *Things Your Mathematics Teacher Should Tell You.* Others will be amazed and motivated by his lecture *The African Contribution To Mathematics.*

To book Robin Walker for your next event, send an email to historicalwalker@yahoo.com

To book John Matthews for your next event, send an email to john_matthews60@hotmail.co.uk

INDEX

Printed in Great Britain
by Amazon

70441970R00075